Comparing Charismatic Leaders' Communication Styles

In examining the presidencies of Barack Obama and Donald Trump, and by extension their communication styles, this book provides a foundation for understanding charismatic leadership and its potent effect on followers.

The book identifies each leader's charismatic leadership attributes, focusing specifically on communication and impression management. It presents a qualitative collection of leader observations and outcomes based on publications and audio and video recordings. By examining two distinctly different leaders, each with evidence of effective, if controversial, outcomes, it shows a spectrum of approaches to mobilizing followers.

This book is suited to students and readers interested in leadership studies, leadership communication, and persuasion.

Tim P. McMahon is Associate Professor of Practice at Creighton University and New York University, USA.

Routledge Focus on Communication Studies

Communicating Aggression in a Megamedia World
Beata Sierocka

Multigenerational Communication in Organizations
Insights from the Workplace
Michael G. Strawser, Stephanie A. Smith and Bridget Rubenking

Participatory Community Inquiry in the Opioid Epidemic
A New Approach for Communities in Crisis
Craig Maier

Democracy, Populism, and Neoliberalism in Ukraine
On the Fringes of the Virtual and the Real
Olga Baysha

War, Peace and Populist Discourse in Ukraine
Olga Baysha

Energy Politics and Discourse in Canada
Probing Progressive Extractivism
Sibo Chen

Celebrity Rhetoric and Sexual Misconduct Cases
Discursive Self-Cleaving
Andrea M. McDonnell

Comparing Charismatic Leaders' Communication Styles
A Study of Presidents Barack Obama and Donald Trump
Tim P. McMahon

For more information about this series, please visit: www.routledge.com/

Comparing Charismatic Leaders' Communication Styles

A Study of Presidents Barack Obama and Donald Trump

Tim P. McMahon

NEW YORK AND LONDON

First published 2025
by Routledge
605 Third Avenue, New York, NY 10158

and by Routledge
4 Park Square, Milton Park, Abingdon, Oxon, OX14 4RN

Routledge is an imprint of the Taylor & Francis Group, an informa business

Library of Congress Cataloging-in-Publication Data
Names: McMahon, Tim P. (Timothy Patrick), 1954– author.
Title: Comparing charismatic leaders' communication styles : a study of presidents Barack Obama and Donald Trump / Tim P. McMahon.
Description: New York, NY : Routledge, 2025. | Series: Routledge focus on communication studies | Includes bibliographical references and index.
Identifiers: LCCN 2024029577 (print) | LCCN 2024029578 (ebook) | ISBN 9781032613024 (hardback) | ISBN 9781032613062 (paperback) | ISBN 9781003463047 (ebook)
Subjects: LCSH: Obama, Barack—Oratory. | Trump, Donald, 1946— Oratory. | Charisma (Personality trait)—Political aspects—United States. | Communication in politics—United States. | Rhetoric—Political aspects— United States. | United States—Politics and government—2009-2017. | United States—Politics and government—2017–2021.
Classification: LCC E907 .M36 2025 (print) | LCC E907 (ebook) | DDC 320.97301/4—dc23/eng/20240716
LC record available at https://lccn.loc.gov/2024029577
LC ebook record available at https://lccn.loc.gov/2024029578

ISBN: 978-1-032-61302-4 (hbk)
ISBN: 978-1-032-61306-2 (pbk)
ISBN: 978-1-003-46304-7 (ebk)

DOI: 10.4324/9781003463047

Typeset in Times New Roman
by Apex CoVantage, LLC

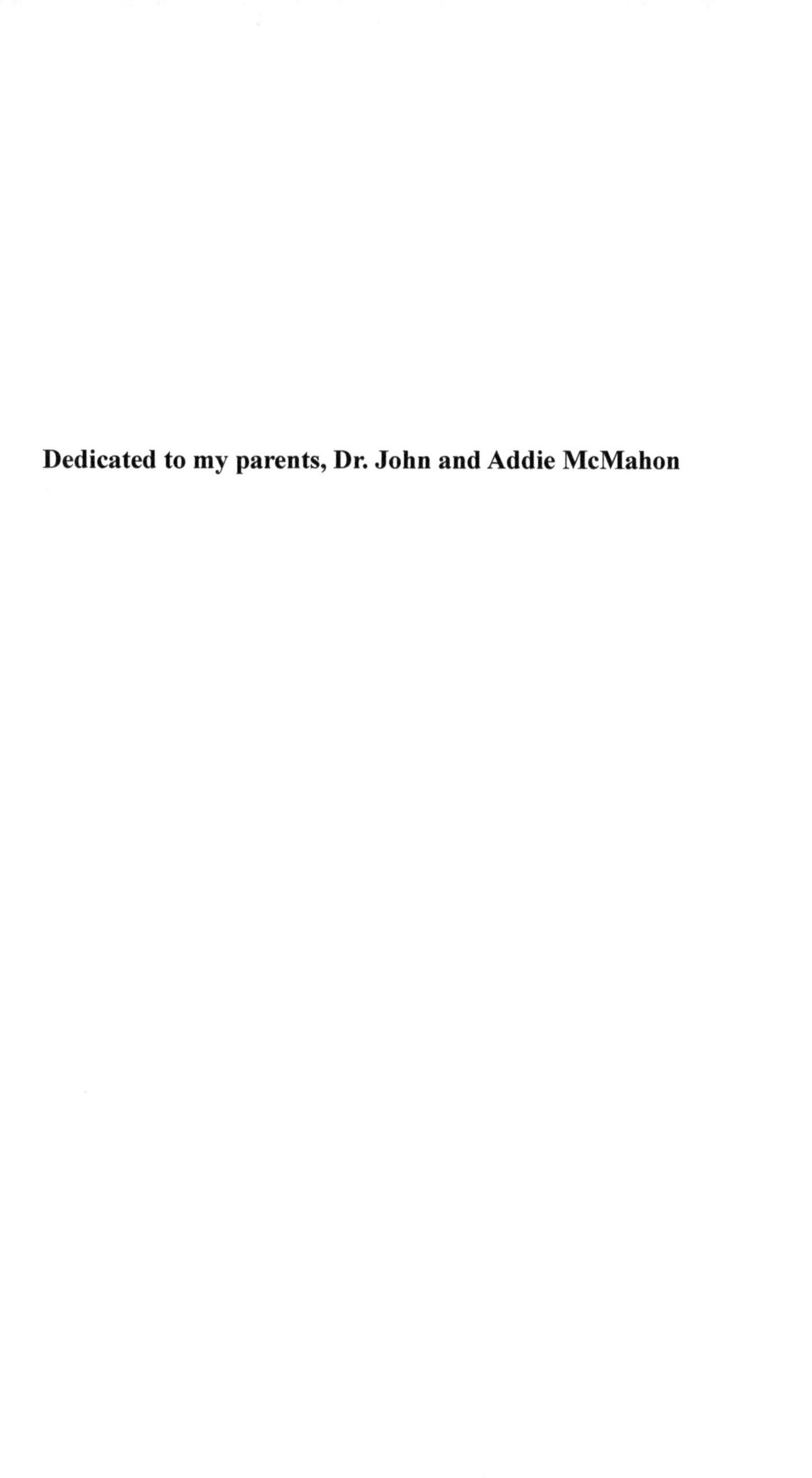

Dedicated to my parents, Dr. John and Addie McMahon

Contents

Acknowledgments

Thanks to my colleagues and students at Creighton University and New York University for their patience and support during the preparation and writing of this book. Special thanks to two world-class designers Dave Webster and Rudy Evans for their expert assistance in preparing the graphics and figures for this book. My eternal gratitude to Debra, my beautiful wife of 50 years.

In writing this book, I made extensive use of Generative AI tools and other cloud-based tools to clarify thinking and communication. My use of these tools is to clarify thoughts, proofread copy, and identify inadvertent errors.

Introduction

Introduction

In modern leadership, charisma continues to be a pivotal force, shaping the destinies of leaders and their followers alike, just as it has since scholars began to study the phenomenon more than 100 years ago. This book explores charismatic leadership through the contrasting styles of Barack Obama and Donald J. Trump, delving into the nuanced realms of personalized and socialized charismatic leadership. At its core, charismatic leadership thrives on the strategic use of communication and rhetoric, tools that these leaders masterfully employ to manage impressions and deeply resonate with the values and beliefs of their followers.

Personalized charismatic leadership (PCL), epitomized by Trump, centers on the leader's magnetic personality and the direct, intense connection with followers. The leader exudes a sense of power and decisiveness, drawing supporters into an alliance of shared convictions that results in uncommon loyalty, yielding unfettered authority to the leader, and emotionally moving followers to act in bold, sometimes risky behavior. Conversely, socialized charismatic leadership (SCL), exemplified by Obama, focuses on collective aspirations and the empowerment of followers, fostering a vision of shared success and mutual advancement that generates spontaneous energy, moving people to act when other leaders have failed to generate a response. That is the magic of charisma—creating powerful commitment from followers—as we present here from opposing perspectives.

This book posits that charismatic leaders possess a keen sense of perceiving the overwrought, though often latent, concerns of segments of the population, along with the leader's adept use of narrative to craft an aura that reflects and shapes adherents' desires and beliefs, generates extraordinary commitment from followers. Moreover, it transforms followers who find possibilities at a time when they believe there are none. Through the lens of Obama's and Trump's political journeys, we examine how charismatic leaders use communication not just as a method of influence but also as the foundation of their charismatic authority.

DOI: 10.4324/9781003463047-1

Through this structured exploration, the book aims to offer a comprehensive analysis of how personalized and socialized charismatic leadership moulded. It is shaped by followers' strategic communication and deep-seated beliefs. It provides insights into the powerful dynamics at play at the highest levels of leadership, which may be effectively applied to personal leadership skills.

Max Weber (1923/1947) considered charisma a form of authority not accessible by ordinary individuals, rather those individuals who "are regarded as of divine origin or as exemplary, and based on . . . [their exceptional qualities] the individual concerned is treated as a leader."[1] Further, charisma is understood as a relationship between leader and followers that unfolds as a source of authority,[2] so it exists in the hearts and minds of followers. Therefore, the attribution of an individual being charismatic stems from followers' uber devotion, characterized by this epigram:

> If a man runs naked down the street proclaiming that he alone can save others from impending doom, and if he immediately wins a following, then he is a charismatic leader. . . . If he does not win a following, he is simply a lunatic.[3]

What follows is a description of each chapter's content. It briefly examines the approach to comparing the two sides of charismatic leadership as viewed through the presidencies of Barack Obama and Donald J. Trump.

Chapter 1 is a review of charismatic leadership premised on the seminal works of leading scholars in the discipline. It provides a brief literature review of applicable research and findings from theories contributing to an understanding of antecedents and effects of the charismatic leadership phenomenon at the highest levels of leadership, with attention to the two contrasting forms, personalized charismatic leadership (PCL) and socialized charismatic leadership (SCL).

Chapters 2 and 3 examine Barack Obama's and Donald J. Trump's charismatic leadership styles. They describe the background leading to each former president's rise, characteristics, leadership styles, and relationships with ardent followers, such as community and religious groups. There is an analysis of the contrasting aspects of Obama's socialized and Trump's personalized forms of charismatic leadership.

Chapter 4 explores the bonds that form between charismatic leaders and their followers through the formation of their relationships, explaining how and why these associations may become intensely potent. It also discusses the role of religious rhetoric and symbolism in fostering followers' fervent loyalty.

Chapter 5 surveys how each leader mobilized their respective political bases of support, the nature of the governing processes employed, and the general effect of each form of charismatic leadership—socialized and personalized—on political discourse.

Chapter 6 presents the benefits and risks of SCL (bright) and PCL (dark) charismatic leadership and explores how different segments of followers view leaders. The potential emotional and psychological the leaders may have had on their followers.

Comparing and contrasting the distinctly different styles of two leaders helps us understand the impact of leadership style on the outcomes and effectiveness of their terms in office. This comparison illuminates how different approaches to leadership can lead to varying results in terms of team performance, organizational success, follower engagement, and overall influence. By examining the contrasting styles, one can identify the strengths and weaknesses of each approach, learn from their successes and failures, the risks and benefits, and apply these insights to develop more effective leadership strategies and practices. Observing charismatic leadership from a multidisciplinary perspective yields a deeper understanding of the phenomenon.

Notes

1 Weber, M. (1923/1947). *The theory of social and economic organizations* (A. M. Henderson, and T. Parsons, Trans.; T. Parsons, Ed.). New York, NY: Free Press, pp. 358–359.
2 One of three enumerated by Weber, the other two being traditional and legal.
3 Wilson, B. (1975). *The noble savages: The Primitive origins of charisma and its contemporary survival.* Berkeley: University of California Press.

Reference List

Weber, M. (1923/1947). *The theory of social and economic organizations* (A. M. Henderson, and T. Parsons, Trans.; T. Parsons, Ed.). New York, NY: Free Press, pp. 358–359.

Wilson, B. (1975). *The noble savages: The primitive origins of charisma and its contemporary survival.* Berkeley: University of California Press.

1 The nature of charisma

For our purposes, we consider two broad perspectives of leadership. One considers a collaborative process, or "an influence relationship among leaders and followers who intend real changes that reflect their mutual purposes."[1] This definition emphasizes the reciprocal and purpose-driven nature of the leader–follower relationship, focusing on mutual intentions for real change, and implies a commonly held purpose embedded in an influence relationship, so "behaviors to persuade other people must be noncoercive."[2]

A second perspective on leadership is more hierarchical. It is driven by a top-down process whereby an individual operating with authority influences and directs the behavior of others toward achieving goals or objectives. In this model, the leader exerts command and control over subordinates, who are expected to follow instructions and policies. While followers may influence messages, communication often flows from the top-down, and decision-making is centralized with the leader or a group of senior leaders. This traditional view of leadership emphasizes structure, order, and clear lines of authority.[3]

With those perspectives, we examine charismatic leadership (CL) as a distinct type of leadership that results in uncommon outcomes and may emanate from a socialized perspective, where the leader emphasizes empowerment, or personalized perspective, in which the leader values control. In Figure 1.1, you will see a depiction of the two faces of CL depicted in the main campaign themes of the two central characters in this book. It serves as a graphic representation of the contrasting examples of charisma.

Historical and theoretical background of charisma

More than 100 years ago, Max Weber (1923/1947) laid the foundation for understanding charismatic leadership as a form of authority based on the leader's exceptional qualities. Scholars have researched charismatic leadership for the last 50 years, developing viable theories to explain its outsized effects on followers. Bruce Avolio (1999)[4] focused on how charismatic leaders inspire and motivate followers to achieve extraordinary outcomes. Bass and Bass (2006)[5] explored how charismatic leaders influence organizational culture and

DOI: 10.4324/9781003463047-2

performance through their vision, inspiration, and values. Jay A. Conger and Rabindra N. Kanungo (1998)[6] advanced charismatic leadership theory (CLT), emphasizing the importance of leaders' personal qualities, impression management, ability to inspire and motivate, emotional intelligence, vision setting, ethical behavior, and the dark side of charismatic leadership.

Robert House (1977)[7] proposed that charismatic appeal is based on the emotional interaction between leaders and followers. Boas Shamir and Jane M. Howell (1999)[8] furthered the development of CLT, particularly concerning the leader–follower relationship, how leaders inspire trust, loyalty, and commitment, and its impact on organizational behavior and outcomes. Gary Yukl (2008)[9] explored how charismatic leaders can influence follower attitudes, behaviors, and performance outcomes, highlighting the potential positive impact of charismatic leadership on organizational success.

Joseph R. Meindl and Sanford Ehrlich (1987)[10] offered that followers attribute exceptional qualities to leaders based on their perceptions of their unique roles or contributions within a specific context and attribute charismatic qualities to leaders when they perceive no one else can perform the role or functions effectively. Finally, R. J. House and J. M. Howell (1992)[11] focused on the psychological aspects of charismatic leadership. They asserted that the need for power, power inhibition, Machiavellianism, authoritarianism, narcissism, self-esteem, and control are likely to differentiate personalized from socialized charismatic leaders.

Figure 1.1 The two faces of charismatic leaders

Advancement of the study of charismatic leadership culminated in a flurry of work nearly two decades ago. The work since that time has brought more clarity and debate on specific aspects of CL. For our purposes in studying the presidencies of two charismatic presidents, four theories serve to inform our understanding of charismatic leadership: (a) transformational theory, (b) self-concept, (c) social contagion, and (d) attribution theory. What follows is a summary of research contributions to these four areas of study to provide a framework for understanding the formation of the two types of charismatic leadership—socialized and personalized.

Regarding *transformational theory,* Burns (1978) developed a model that distinguishes motivation based on two types of leadership: transactional and transformational. In a transactional environment, the leader provides followers with something they want in return for something the leader wants, often seen in business and bureaucratic environments with clear lines of responsibility. With transformational, leaders raise the interests of their followers, transforming their values and self-concepts and motivating them to extraordinary levels of performance by providing a sense of vision and mission, often aligning followers' values and goals with that of the organization.

These findings led to further studies discovering the importance of the leaders' communication skills being uniquely tied to charisma and its effect on follower confidence (Bass, 1996), a concept Bryman (1992) believed was more attributable to inspiration. Bass and Avolio (1993) developed a model of four critical behavioral components (e.g., idealized influence, inspiration, intellectual stimulation, and individualized consideration), leading to two quantitative instruments based on follower ratings of leaders that are inherently based on perception. Some scholars posited that followers' ratings of leadership effectiveness were more closely tied to their satisfaction rather than the leader's charisma. This work established that followers are engaged and moved to act when the leader articulates a vision that squarely addresses deep concerns. Transformational leadership profoundly impacts followers, often leading to significant positive changes in their performance, motivation, engagement, and satisfaction.

In *Self-concept Theory,* House (1977) believed that charismatic leadership transforms followers' self-concepts and achieves its motivational outcomes by altering followers' perceptions of work, offering an appealing vision, developing collective identity among followers, and expanding self-confidence. Shamir et al. (1993) discovered that leaders who articulate a shared vision stimulate confidence in followers' belief that they can realize extraordinary outcomes. Building a model that could test and advance clear thinking on this premise (House, 1977; Yukl, 2006) led to the recognition of the power of a leader's vision, conviction, and bold statements bolstered by their perceived personal sacrifice caused followers in the relationship to adhere tightly to the shared values and vision, thereby making sense of the situation and furthering commitment to the challenge at hand. Conger and Kanungo (1998) summarized the key elements of leader behavior upon which there is universal agreement: (1) vision, (2) inspiration, (3) meaning-making, (4) empowerment, (5) setting of high expectations, and (6) fostering collective identity.[12]

To summarize, self-concept theory significantly impacts the leader–follower dynamic, influencing how leaders and followers view themselves and each other. This mutual perception shapes their interactions, affects their roles' effectiveness, and determines the success of their collective endeavors. Leaders who understand and engage with the self-concepts of themselves and their followers are more likely to create positive, productive, and transformative relationships.

While not at the heart of charismatic leadership, *social contagion theory* adds perspective to understanding how followers who may have never had a personal encounter with a charismatic leader have become enchanted with their charisma. This effect was particularly evident in social and religious movements and radical political parties. Meindl (1985) offered that followers socially construct the meaning they derive from leaders. Further, Shamir (2007) discovered that members of these movements attribute power and causality to leaders to understand and act appropriately in an environment of doubt or uncertainty. In other words, they influence one another by giving into their inhibitions as they grow confident they are not alone in their views, affirming their latent intent is morally superior (Yukl, 2006).

While the heroic nature of charismatic leaders attracts us, James R. Meindl (1995) offered that people tend to overestimate the impact of leadership on organizational outcomes, often attributing heroic or charismatic qualities to leaders based on the success or failure of their organizations. His research points to the social construction of leadership, proposing that our understanding of charismatic leadership is heavily influenced by cultural, situational, and psychological factors that lead followers to ascribe extraordinary capabilities and qualities to leaders. This attribution process can enhance a leader's perceived charisma, regardless of their behaviors or performance. Social contagion accelerates the attribution of charisma to a leader as a form of collective behavior or shared emotional experience, mainly when ideas are discrepant from accepted social norms.

These scholars—Pastor et al. (2007)—connected the social construction of leadership with the contagion model, [13] verifying that the attribution of charisma to a leader was more dependent upon social networks than actual leader behavior. Further, Antonakis and Atwater (2002) built on the nuanced understanding of close and distant relationships by re-imagining the physical distance between leader and follower, which could be considered alternately in two dimensions: physical and hierarchical. In other words, when people are physically close, they have more opportunities for direct interaction, leading to stronger social bonds and more immediate and tangible social constructs.

Conversely, physical distance can lead to a reliance on mediated forms of communication, potentially creating different social dynamics and interpretations. Hierarchies establish roles, power dynamics, and expectations within a group or organization, significantly affecting social interaction. Individuals in higher hierarchical positions often have the power to shape norms, values, and beliefs within the group, which others then internalize and reproduce. Those in subordinate positions may have their behavior and perceptions shaped by the expectations and actions of their superiors. Both physical and hierarchical relationships contribute to the context in which social meaning is created. They can dictate the flow of information, the formality of interactions, and the extent to which individuals identify with a group or its leaders. Moreover, they can reinforce or challenge existing social structures and cultural norms, influencing how reality is collectively constructed and understood.

Social contagion theory significantly impacts the leader–follower relationship by highlighting how leaders' emotions, behaviors, and values can spread. Leaders aware of their influence can harness this phenomenon to foster positive change and develop a healthy organizational culture, ultimately leading to enhanced group cohesion and improved performance.

Attribution theory, which focuses on how individuals interpret events and how this relates to their thinking and behavior, has profound implications for the leader–follower relationship. This theory examines how people attribute causes to behaviors and outcomes—whether they see them as internally caused (due to personal traits or choices) or externally caused (due to situational factors). From a communication point of view, the theory considers "the internal (thinking) and external (talking) process of interpreting and understanding what is behind our own and others' behaviors."[14] Specifically, this perspective is a means to explain why individual and social events happen. With respect to charismatic leadership, Conger and Kanungo (1987) discovered that when followers could put into context the leader's attitudes and beliefs about vision and goals, the result was high levels of intrinsic motivation in the group.

For example, as has been realized in other studies, the attribution of charisma depends on recognizing the leader articulating a discrepant view contrary to the status quo. When it resonates with individuals, they attribute charismatic authority to the leader. Several factors contribute to the efficacy of the application of this theory. When followers recognized that the leader had paid a price (self-sacrifice) to accomplish the vision, followers attributed trust and confidence in the leader. In another study, Conger and Kanungo (1998) determined evidence of crisis was not necessary for this attribution to occur, a condition Weber (1923/1947) believed was required. The difference may lie in the interpretation of the presence of a crisis. In this book, a crisis is present when those involved feel a significant threat exists to the fundamental values, goals, or functioning of an organization, society, or individual and may appear as a threat to physical safety, financial stability, or critical infrastructure.

In summary, attribution theory provides a means to understanding leader–follower interactions. Through the eyes of the leader, attributions they make to followers may significantly affect their subsequent interactions with followers, perhaps causing them to clarify their perception of the situation and take necessary action. From a follower perspective, attributions ascribed to leaders can significantly affect their subsequent interactions. That is, if a leader's actions are perceived to be based on the personal gain of the leader, their job satisfaction and subsequent commitment may wane. Leaders and followers can foster a more supportive, effective, and empathetic organizational environment by being mindful of how attributions are formed and communicated. This awareness helps build trust, enhance motivation, and effectively manage conflicts, ultimately contributing to better organizational outcomes.

By 1996, charismatic leadership became the "predominant paradigm in organizational leadership theory and research," according to J. Bryan Fuller.[15] It was so dominant that researchers became blind to the harmful effects of charismatic leadership. They cited the contrasts between two categories of recognized charismatics, Dr. Martin Luther King and Adolph Hitler. King moved his followers to push for needed social change. In contrast, Hitler used his charisma to commit evil acts.[16] (House & Howell, 1992) coined the term personalized charismatic leadership (PCL) to describe the opposing side and socialized charismatic leadership (SCL) to describe the positive. Personalized leaders act to benefit themselves, whereas socialized leaders benefit the collective interests of followers. Both leaders crave power, however, for different purposes.

Expanding on this duality, Tomas Chamorro-Premuzic asserts that charisma is rooted in emotional manipulation with the potential to lead followers "to abandon rational thought and accept ideas uncritically."[17] Additionally, "charismatic leaders tend to become 'addicted' to the unquestioning approval of their followers, which distorts their judgment and distracts them from their goals."[18] Followers, in turn, "become addicted to the leader's charisma . . . [resulting] in a 'reciprocal dependence' that leads both parties to 'distort reality.'"[19]

McClelland (1985) generalized that behavioral charisma[20] is an interactive function based on the leader's nonconscious needs for power, achievement, and affiliation. House et al. (1991)[21] hypothesized that charisma is positively related to a need for power[22] and negatively related to the need for achievement and affiliation, which their study of presidents confirmed. Leaders attract followers high on one or more of these elements. In summary, influential leaders, through their values, personal example, enthusiasm, and confidence, provide followers with a need for cohesion, inspiration, and fundamental values. They termed this phenomenon behavioral charisma and cautioned that it could result in destructive behavior in the wrong hands.

This chapter explores the multifaceted nature of charismatic leadership, tracing its evolution from Weber's foundational concept to modern theories emphasizing vision, inspiration, and ethical behavior. It contrasts the positive, transformative SCL with the more self-serving PCL, examining how such leaders impact follower motivation and organizational outcomes. Theories discussed included transformational leadership, which motivates by aligning followers and organizational values, and attribution theory, focusing on follower perceptions of leadership. Social contagion theory's role in charisma is acknowledged, along with the dangers of charisma, like emotional manipulation and reality distortion.

Behavioral characteristics of charismatic leaders

Charismatic leaders possess distinctive behavioral characteristics that set them apart and enable them to exert a heartfelt influence on their followers. These leaders exude confidence and are rewarded by followers who grant them authority to pursue their shared vision of the future. They command attention whenever they speak or enter a room. Their communication style is not just articulate but also deeply persuasive, capable of conveying complex ideas in a way that is accessible and inspiring to others. They are adept storytellers who connect with people emotionally, delivering compelling narratives that resonate with the hopes and aspirations of their audience.

Charismatic leaders are known for their visionary thinking. They communicate a clear, compelling vision of the future with conviction and passion. This vision is achievable and within reach. They motivate followers to move beyond individual interests. In 1961, President John Kennedy launched the idea of man going to the moon before the decade's end. It represented an ideal to pursue an unexplored frontier, a concept that epitomized the American experience. It also represented risks and costs and required the sacrifice of its people. Kennedy's dream captured the nation's imagination and the hearts and minds with a sense of purpose to literally reach for the stars.

Equipped with a kind of empathy that permits them to understand, if not necessarily share, the feelings of human beings, charismatic leaders relate to people from various backgrounds. They demonstrate concern for their followers' well-being and development through their behavior. The socialized type demonstrates compassion that fosters a strong emotional bond. The personalized type can relate to and articulate followers' feelings, demonstrating understanding rather than compassion. This recognition is sufficient enough to draw the follower closer to that leader.

Winston Churchill, prime minister of Great Britain during World War II, acquired an acute understanding of the problems facing his country. He saw Nazi Germany as an imminent threat, and he worked to prepare his country to act. When war broke out, he acted decisively, making strategic and tactical decisions to defeat the Axis powers, often in a paucity of details. His charisma was evident in his speeches and demeanor—his wit, his defiance, and his capacity to connect with the ordinary citizens and influential figures of his time. He was known for his humor, human engagement, and energy, symbolizing British tenacity.

These kinds of leaders quickly adapt to change, operating on limited information. They are resilient. They see obstacles as opportunities to innovate and grow. They build trust through consistent actions and unwavering convictions. Socialized leaders build loyalty by empowering followers, while the personalized kind exhibits decisiveness, clearing a path of safety to follow. Both types manage followers' expectations through impression management and foster the perception of ethical conduct through their followers' eyes. Socialized leaders value open communication and collaboration, creating an environment where followers understand their role and feel empowered to contribute. Personalized leaders demonstrate behaviors that inspire trust, devotion, and a solid commitment to the group's objectives, leading to the possibility of achieving the change and achievements they seek.

They are exceptional communicators who:

- Convey messages that resonate with their audience's emotions and values.
- Take personal risks and make unconventional decisions to pursue their vision and are not afraid to act boldly.

- Are hyper-attuned to the environment and keep their followers' needs and feelings in sight at all times. This enables them to "feel their pain" and connect with them deeper.
- Identify with followers who believe the leader understands and values them personally.
- Exhibit unconventional behavior. This helps them be seen as change agents with the kind of radical ideas that impassion followers, who, in turn, set them apart from the bureaucrat or professional manager.
- Are assertive and highly confident, reinforcing their position as leaders and inspiring confidence among followers.
- They inspire followers to perform beyond expectations, leading to greater levels of commitment and effort among group members.

They are magnetic. Their messages are often stark and compelling and strike a chord with their audience, igniting followers' emotions and alignment with shared values. They see risk as not a threat but an opportunity to stand out, so they embrace it, making bold and frame-breaking decisions in pursuit of a grand vision.

They exhibit emotional sensitivity that allows for a profound connection based on a mutual understanding of the situation at hand. Breaking from tradition is a hallmark that embellishes their distinctiveness and bolsters their status as remarkable and visionary figures.

Self-confident and forceful, they are ever-present in public scenarios, instilling a sense of trust and belief in their direction among those they lead. By setting high expectations and believing in the role of their followers in accomplishing their objectives, charismatic leaders can inspire those around them to reach new heights of performance and dedication, often exceeding what was thought possible and, when left unchecked, drifting into over-reaction. This synergy between leader and follower intensifies commitment and paves the way for extraordinary achievements.

Conger and Kanungo's charismatic leadership model strongly emphasizes these behavioral and attitudinal aspects that enable leaders to inspire, influence, and drive change within organizations or social movements. Their research suggests that charisma is not merely an innate trait but can be understood and developed as a set of behaviors and strategies that enhance leadership effectiveness.

The contrasting aspects of charisma: personalized and socialized

Generally, we consider charisma an illuminating presence that positively affects the world. We think of a romantic characterization in various fields: in business, Steve Jobs; in social movements, Greta Thunberg; in entertainment, Oprah Winfrey; and in sport, Cristiano Ronaldo. Yet charisma has a dark side, countermanding the conventional perspective that charisma is an endearing, uplifting quality. S. J. Musser (1987) suggested, "We might even classify charismatic leaders as positive or negative by their orientation toward satisfying their own needs versus those of their followers."[23]

As previously referenced, House and Howell (1992) identified that "socialized charismatic leaders have a high need for power, balance with activity inhibition,[24] low authoritarianism, an internal locus of control, high esteem, and low Machiavellianism."[25] A personalized charismatic "leader has a high need for power that is instead coupled with low activity inhibition, high authoritarianism, an external locus of control, low self-esteem, high narcissism, and a high Machiavellianism."[26] In Figure 1.2, see a side-by-side comparison of the differing characteristics of these two forms of CL.

Machiavellianism is a personality trait characterized by manipulation and deceit. It is named after the Italian Renaissance diplomat Niccolo Machiavelli. Machiavellian thought is characterized by a manipulative and exploitative attitude toward others, a lack of empathy, and a cynical view of human nature. Its positive aspects include its benefits in negotiation and short-term situations.

Kenneth Goodpaster (2007) introduced the idea of teleopathy to the discussion of ethics. He defined it as "the unbalanced pursuit of goals or purposes by an individual or an organized group."[27] He identifies three symptoms of its presence: fixation or singleness of purpose under stress, rationalization, and detachment. One builds on the other and may create a suspension of ethical awareness as different criteria take over thoughts. He wrote: "Business leaders are the architects of corporate conscience. . . . Delivering on the moral agenda is their

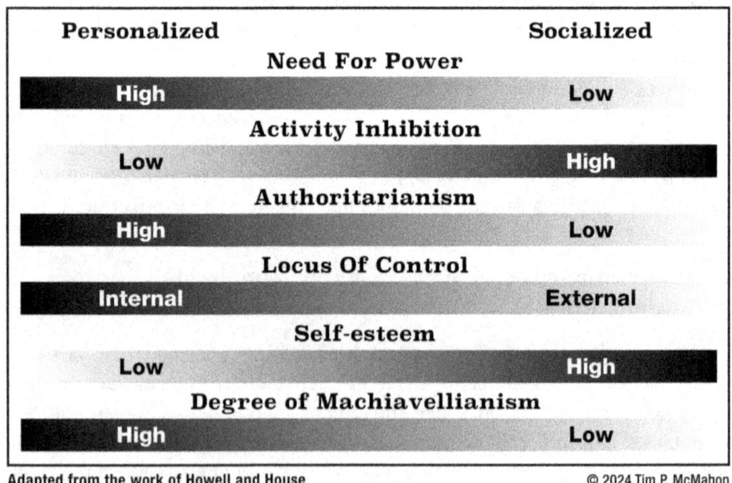

Figure 1.2 The spectrum of charismatic leadership

responsibility. Enlightenment and courage must walk hand in hand."[28] Does this ethical description give rise to a judgment about charismatic leaders—whether personalized or socialized? It would seem that the healthy practice of ethics would be more likely to be present with socialized charismatic leaders.

Notes

1 Rost, J. C. (1991). *Leadership for the twenty-first century*. Westport, CT; London, UK: Praeger.
2 Ibid, (p. 105).
3 Taylor, F. W. (1947). *Scientific management*. New York, NY; London, UK: Harper & Brothers.
4 Avolio, B. J. (1999). *Full leadership development: Building the vital forces in organizations*. Thousand Oaks, CA: SAGE.
5 Bass, B. M., and Bass, R. B. (2006). *The bass handbook of leadership* (4th ed.). New York, NY: The Free Press.
6 Conger, J. A., and Kanungo, R. N. (1998). *Charismatic leadership in organizations*. Thousand Oaks, CA: SAGE.
7 House, R. J. (1977). A theory of charismatic leadership. In J. G. Hunt, and L. L. Larson (Eds.), *Leadership: The cutting edge*. Carbondale, IL: Southern Illinois University Press.
8 Shamir, B., and Howell, J. M. (1999). Organizational and contextual influences on the emergence and effectiveness of charismatic leadership. *The Leadership Quarterly*, 10(2), 257–283.
9 Yukl, G. (2008). How leaders influence organizational effectiveness. *The Leadership Quarterly*, 19(6), 708–722.
10 Meindl, J. R., and Ehrlich, S. B. (1987). The romance of leadership and the evaluation of organizational performance. *Academy of Management Journal*, 30(1), 91–109.
11 House, R. J., and Howell, J. M. (1992). Personality and charismatic leadership. *The Leadership Quarterly*, 2(3).
12 Conger and Kanungo (1998), (p. 19).
13 Social contagion theory states that individuals can be influenced by the actions, emotions, and ideas of others, leading to a form of collective behavior or shared emotional experience that spreads through groups and communities much like that of a contagious disease.
14 Manusov, V., and Spitzberg, B. (2008). Attribution theory. In L. A. Baxter, and D. O. Braithwaite (Eds.), *Engaging theories in interpersonal communication: Multiple perspectives*. Thousand Oaks, CA: SAGE, p. 37.
15 Fuller, J. B., Patterson, C. E. P., Hester, K., and Stringer, D. Y. (1996, February). A quantitative review of research on charismatic leadership. *Psychological Reports*, 78(1), 271–287.
16 House, R. J. and Howell, J. M. (1992). Personality and charismatic leadership. *The Leadership Quarterly*, (3)2, 1992.
17 Shonk, K. T. (2023, December 14). Charismatic leadership: Weighing the pros and cons. *Harvard Law School Daily Blog*. https://www.pon.harvard.edu/daily/leadership-skills-daily/charismatic-leadership-weighing-the-pros-and-cons/.
18 Ibid.

19 Ibid.
20 Charisma based on actual or perceived behavior of the leader.
21 House, R. J., Spangler, W. D., and Wocyke, J. (1991, September). Personality and charisma in the U.S. presidency: A psychological theory of leader effectiveness. *Administrative Science Quarterly,* 364–396.
22 Activity inhibition refers to the ability of an individual to inhibit or restrain their impulses, behaviors, and immediate reactions in response to external stimuli or internal emotions. It involves self-control and the capacity to regulate one's actions, particularly in situations requiring patience, deliberation, or adherence to social norms and rules. In the context of personality psychology, activity inhibition is often discussed as a trait that helps in managing and moderating behavior to fit into social expectations and achieve long-term goals.
23 Conger and Kanungo referenced S. J. Musser in their 1998 book on charismatic leadership. Conger and Kanungo (1998), (p. 212).
24 Activity inhibition refers to a leader's self-control and the restraint they show in their actions and behaviors. Leaders with high activity inhibition are typically more deliberate and thoughtful in their responses to situations, refraining from impulsive actions. They tend to be disciplined, able to delay gratification, and may be more cautious and risk-averse.
25 Ibid, (p. 212).
26 Ibid.
27 Goodpaster, K. E. (2007). *Conscious and corporate culture*. Malden, MA: Blackwell Publishing, p. xiii.
28 Ibid, (p. xv).

Reference List

Antonakis, J., and Atwater, L. (2002). Leader distance: A review and a proposed theory. *The Leadership Quarterly*, 13(6), 673–704. https://doi.org/10.1016/S1048-9843(02)00155-8.

Avolio, B. J. (1999). *Full leadership development: Building the vital forces in organizations*.Thousand Oaks, CA: SAGE.

Bass, B. M. (1996). *A new paradigm of leadership: An inquiry into transformational leadership. U.S.* Alexandria, VA: Army Research Institute for the Behavioral and Social Sciences.

Bass, B. M., & Avolio, B. J. (1993). Transformational Leadership and Organizational Culture. *Public Administration Quarterly*, 17, 112–121.

Bass, B. M., and Bass, R. B. (2006). *The bass handbook of leadership* (4th ed.). New York, NY: The Free Press.

Bryman, A. E. (1992). *Charisma & leadership*. London, U.K./ Newbury, CA. SAGE.

Conger, J. A. and Kanungo, R. B. (1987). Charismatic leadership in organizations: Perceived behavioral attributes and their measurement. *Journal of Orgnizaional Behavior*, 15(5), 439–452. (September, 1994).

Conger, J. A., and Kanungo, R. N. (1998). *Charismatic leadership in organizations*. Thousand Oaks, CA: SAGE.

Fuller, J. B., Patterson, C. E. P., Hester, K., and Stringer, D. Y. (1996, February). A quantitative review of research on charismatic leadership. *Psychological Reports*, 78(1), 271–287.

Goodpaster, K. E. (2007). *Conscious and corporate culture*. Malden, MA: Blackwell Publishing.

House, R. J. (1977). A theory of charismatic leadership. In J. G. Hunt, and L. L. Larson (Eds.), *Leadership: The cutting edge*. Carbondale, IL: Southern Illinois University Press.

House, R. J., and Howell, J. M. (1992). Personality and charismatic leadership. *The Leadership Quarterly,* 2(3).

House, R. J., Spangler, W. D., and Wocyke, J. (1991, September). Personality and charisma in the U.S. presidency: A psychological theory of leader effectiveness. *Administrative Science Quarterly,* 364–396.

Manusov, V., and Spitzberg, B. (2008). Attribution theory. In L. A. Baxter, and D. O. Braithwaite (Eds.), *Engaging theories in interpersonal communication: Multiple perspectives*. Thousand Oaks, CA: SAGE.

McClelland, D. C. (1985). How Motives, Skills, and Values Determine What People Do. *American Psychologist*, 40, 812–825. https://doi.org/10.1037/0003-066X.40.7.812.

Meindl, J. R. (1995). The romance of leadership as a follower-centric theory: A social constructionist approach. *The Leadership Quarterly*, 6(3), 329–341. https://doi.org/10.1016/1048-9843(95)90012-8.

Meindl, J. R., and Ehrlich, S. B. (1987). The romance of leadership and the evaluation of organizational performance. *Academy of Management Journal,* 30(1), 91–109.

Meindl, J. R., Ehrlich, S. B., and Dukerich, J. M. (1985). The romance of leadership. *Adm Sci Q*, 30, 78–102.

Pastor, J. C., Mayo, M., and Shamir, B. *Journal of Applied Psychology*, Vol 92(6), Nov 2007, 1584–1596.

Rost, J. C. (1991). *Leadership for the twenty-first century*. Westport, CT; London, UK: Praeger.

Shamir, B. (2007). From passive recipients to active co-producers: Followers' roles in the leadership process. Follower-centered perspectives on leadership: A tribute to the memory of James R. Meindl, 9, 39.

Shamir, B., and Howell, J. M. (1999). Organizational and contextual influences on the emergence and effectiveness of charismatic leadership. *The Leadership Quarterly,* 10(2), 257–283.

Shamir, B., Robert J. House, Michael B. Arthur. (1993). The Motivational Effects of Charismatic Leadership: A Self-Concept Based Theory. *Organization Science*, 4(4), 577–594.

Shonk, K. T. (2023, December 14). Charismatic leadership: Weighing the pros and cons. *Harvard Law School Daily Blog*. https://www.pon.harvard.edu/daily/leadership-skills-daily/charismatic-leadership-weighing-the-pros-and-cons/.

Taylor, F. W. (1947). *Scientific management*. New York, NY; London, UK: Harper & Brothers.

Weber, M. (1923/1947). *The theory of social and economic organizations* (A. M. Henderson, and T. Parsons, Trans.; T. Parsons, Ed.). New York, NY: Free Press, pp. 358–359.

Yukl, G. (2008). How leaders influence organizational effectiveness. *The Leadership Quarterly,* 19(6).

2 Barack Obama's charismatic leadership

Background and rise to prominence

Barack Hussein Obama, born on August 4, 1961, in Honolulu, Hawaii, is an American politician and attorney who served as the 44th President of the United States from 2009 to 2017. He is noted for being the first African American to hold the presidency.

A multicultural upbringing marked Obama's early life. He was born to a Kenyan father, Barack Obama Sr., and an American mother, Stanley Ann Dunham. His parents met while attending the University of Hawaii. After his father returned to his homeland in Kenya, his mother married an Indonesian man, and Obama spent part of his childhood in Jakarta, Indonesia, before returning to Hawaii to live with his maternal grandparents. At the time, he would enter fifth grade.

In Hawaiian culture, the school you attended had much to do with one's status and perceived self-worth. Nine out of ten applicants to Punahou School, Hawaii's oldest, largest, and most prestigious private school, were rejected. Yet Barry, as he was known at the time, was accepted. His admission was the result of

> the persistence of his mother, who was tireless at working the system, even from afar; his winning performance during interviews with the administration office; a need-based scholarship program that had begun targeting students of his potential and diverse background; and the influence of two wealthy alumni.[1]

Obama later acknowledged that his "admission into Punahou heralded the start of something grand, an elevation in the family status that they took great pains to let everyone know."[2] Yet, unlike his previous home in Jakarta, Indonesia, where Westerners were considered the wealthy class, in "Honolulu many native Hawaiian bouts displayed a prove-it-yourself-or-else hostility toward people with roots on the mainland, known as haole."[3]

DOI: 10.4324/9781003463047-3

Biographers maintain Obama was shaped by both nature and nurture. Three family elders influenced his development, including his mother, Stanley Ann, or simply Ann, his maternal grandmother, Madelyn Dunham (née Madelyn Lee Payne), and his maternal grandfather, Stanley Dunham. As mentioned, his parents divorced, and his father returned to his birthplace in Kenya. Although the marriage was short-lived, the cultural and racial diversity of the senior Obama's heritage shaped his son's early understanding of the world. His father "had a captivating voice, a mesmerizing presence, a certainty that he was correct, and a love of argument."[4]

His mother was inclined to find the best in every person she met, especially people from different places and cultures.[5] Ann's career as an anthropologist took her and young Barack, whom she called Barry or "Bar," pronounced "Bear," to Indonesia. There, she immersed herself in village life and studied the local crafts, economy, and social dynamics. This experience exposed young Obama to new cultural and religious traditions, fostering an early appreciation for diversity and global perspectives. Ann was resilient and determined, pursuing her career and education while raising Obama. She woke him early in the mornings for English lessons, instilling in him the value of discipline and the pursuit of knowledge. Her rigorous standards of scholarship and ethics left an indelible mark on Obama, shaping his academic and later political aspirations.

Ann also conveyed a deep sense of empathy and social justice to Obama through her work. She often worked with marginalized communities, focusing on women's roles in the local economy and advocating for their rights and welfare. These experiences, shared through her stories and values, helped Obama develop a keen sense of social responsibility and a desire to effect change. Her influence was profound and multifaceted. Her intellectual curiosity, commitment to social justice, and global outlook were integral to shaping the future president.

Obama reflected on his mother's life lessons in *A Promised Land,* one of his autobiographies, recalling an incident in which his mother discovered he was one of a group of boys teasing another student. She told him, "there are people in the world who think about themselves. They don't care what happens to others as long as they get what they want. They put other people down to make themselves feel important,"[6] Obama said while she was highly disappointed in his behavior, viewing the event as a teaching moment. "Then there are people who do the opposite, who can imagine how others must feel and make sure that they don't do things that hurt people. . . . Which kind of person do you want to be?"[7] Obama acknowledged that the question had stayed with him for a long time.

Madelyn Dunham, his grandmother, played a pivotal role in his upbringing, proving stability while nurturing and shaping his character and values. Obama called her "Toot," short for *tutu,* a Hawaiian term for "grandparent," as she was highly influential in his life. She imbued him with her strength and discipline while providing a loving presence. Having grown up in the Midwest, she embodied values of hard work, responsibility, and pragmatism. She was a force in the business world, breaking the glass ceilings of her time and rising to vice president at the bank. She demonstrated to Obama the importance of determination and equality in the workplace. She earned respect from her employer and other influential people, two of whom vouched for Barack's acceptance at Punahou.

Madelyn instilled in him respect for others, discipline of self, and the value of education. Obama reflected that "In tough spots, I tend to channel my grandmother."[8] He wrote of her and her family: "These were sensible people who worked hard, went to church, paid their bills, and remained suspicious of bombast, public displays of emotion, or foolishness of a sort."[9] Madelyn was strict but caring, ensuring Obama completed his homework and maintained good grades. She demanded academic excellence as it was an earmark of the discipline and the importance of striving for one's goals. This greatly influenced Obama, fostering a sense of responsibility and self-discipline that would later define his career and presidency.

Moreover, her experiences during the racially charged periods of American history combined with her work in banking—unusual for a woman at the time—provided Obama with a nuanced understanding of race and gender issues and influenced his views on equality and social justice. Her pragmatic approach to life's challenges and her sense of fairness shaped Obama's worldview—a balanced and sensible approach to decision-making reflecting his deep belief in the American values of hard work leading to upward mobility.

Stanley Armour Dunham was his grandfather. Stanley was a charismatic and adventurous figure who captured Obama's attention and embedded him with a sense of adventure, particularly in his early years. Stanly had a larger-than-life personality, was an entertaining storyteller, and was somewhat unconventional. He served in the Army during World War II and freely shared his exploits during the war. His adventurous spirit greatly influenced his yarns. These narratives often blended fact with fiction but were instrumental in sparking Obama's imagination and curiosity about the world.

Stanley's relationship with Obama was characterized by fun and adventure. He often took Obama on various excursions, exposing him to many experiences that broadened his perspective of human nature. The younger Barack developed a sense of openness and curiosity, later defining his personal and political life approach. While playful and easygoing, the elder Obama provided a sense of security and belonging that was crucial during Obama's formative years, helping him navigate the challenges of adolescence and identity formation. Further, his experiences with racial discrimination, especially during his military service and in his personal life, formed an understanding of race and social justice issues in his grandson. Stanley's stories and attitudes toward race and equality helped shape Obama's awareness of social and racial dynamics, influencing his commitment to civil rights and social justice later in life.

Obama was raised chiefly "in Hawaii soaking up the serene environment of the tropical island in the Pacific—playing basketball, bodysurfing and socializing with friends."[10] Barack's upbringing was full of rich experiences and strong characters. "The effects of his childhood in Hawaii and Indonesia are . . . readily evident in the adult Obama, his uncommon combination of cool remove and adaptability."[11]

His adolescent years permitted self-discovery in that he "grew up without his father, with his mother often gone, and in a sense raised himself, working his way alone through many confounding issues life threw his way."[12] He was preoccupied with avoiding life's traps, in his case, his unusual family biography, his childhood geography (being situated in a remote part of the world, Hawaii, and formative years in Jakarta), "[a]nd finally the trap of race in America, with its likelihood of rejection and cynicism."[13]

He completed his high school education in Hawaii and then moved to the mainland United States to attend Occidental College in Los Angeles for two years. He transferred to Columbia University in New York City, graduating in 1983 with a Bachelor of Arts in political science. After working in the business sector for a few years, Obama moved to Chicago, where he became involved in community organizing.

In 1988, Obama enrolled at Harvard Law School. He became the first African American president of the Harvard Law Review, a prestigious legal journal. After earning his Juris Doctor degree, magna cum laude, in 1991, he returned to Chicago. He practiced as a civil rights attorney and taught constitutional law at the University of Chicago Law School.

It was the two years he spent at Occidental College in Los Angeles that "represented the start of political awakening."[14] He had a jaded view of politicians, writing,

With few exceptions, everything I observed about politicians seemed dubious:

> the blow-dried hair, the wolfish grins, the bromides and self-peddling on TV while behind closed doors they curried favor of corporations and other monied interests. They were actors in a rigged game, I decided, and I wanted no part of it.[15]

What captured his attention were social movements, studying Gandhi, Lech Walesa, and especially young civil rights leaders like Dr. Martin Luther King, John Lewis, Bob Moses, Fannie Lou Hamer, and Diane Nash. He saw in them the lessons his mother taught him about how "you could build power not by putting others down but by lifting them up."[16] He saw them as the essence of democracy at work, not the demagoguery. He viewed demagogues as those who appealed to popular beliefs by arousing fears, exaggerating dangers, and preying on emotions through fiery oratory.

Pursuing this acquired understanding of how the world worked led him to transfer to Columbia University, where he lived "like a monk—reading, writing, filling up journals, rarely bothering with college parties or even eating hot meals."[17] He admitted that this period of intense reflection, asking questions like why some movements succeed, and others fail, awakened his interest in making a mark on the world. It was his metanoia.

Obama entered politics when he ran for and was elected to the Illinois State Senate in 1996, representing the 13th district. During his tenure in the state legislature, he worked on legislation reforming ethics and healthcare laws. He served three terms until 2004. During his tenure there, Obama learned that change was hard to accomplish. Being in the minority party, he could see how Illinois Republicans behaved like Newt Gingrich on the national level, exercising "absolute control over what bills got out of committee and which amendments were in order."[18]

Reflecting on his experiences, Obama related a story about a passionate argument based on solid conservative logic protesting a bill that "proposed a blatant tax giveaway to some favored industry when the state was cutting services to the poor."[19] When he finished, the senate president made his way to Obama's desk, complimented him on his speech, and said, "That was a hell of a speech, made some good points. . . . Might have even changed a few minds, but didn't change any votes."[20] The bill easily passed. Obama observed that most legislation was opaque. Legislators made dispassionate political calculations, "all the while keeping a careful eye on the handful of ideological hot buttons—guns, abortion, taxes—that might generate heat from their base."[21]

In the prologue of his first autobiography, he wrote:

> Someone once said that every man is trying to either live up to his father's expectations or make up for his father's mistakes, and I suppose that may explain my particular malady as well as anything else.[22]

Overview of Obama's leadership skills, accomplishments, and public persona

Obama's rise to national prominence began with his keynote address at the Democratic National Convention in July 2004. His speech, which emphasized themes of unity and hope, garnered national attention and praise. Later that year, he was elected to the US Senate with 70% of the vote, the most significant margin of victory in Illinois history.[23]

During his tenure in the US Senate, from 2005 to 2008, he held assignments on the Senate committees, including Foreign Relations, Health, Education, Labor, and Pensions; Homeland Security and Governmental Affairs; and Veterans Affairs. He was also a member of the Black Caucus. He demonstrated a keen interest in ethics and government transparency, spearheading the effort to pass the Federal Funding Accountability and Transparency Act of 2006 with Senator Tom Coburn, a Republican from Oklahoma. This legislation was significant for creating a searchable database of federal government spending, aiming to increase transparency and reduce wasteful expenditure. On foreign policy, Obama was proactive in addressing global issues, notably working on nuclear non-proliferation and security. He collaborated with Senator Richard Lugar, a Republican from Indiana, on a bill to enhance the United States' ability to track and secure weapons of mass destruction globally. This bipartisan effort, known as the Lugar–Obama initiative, demonstrated his commitment to addressing critical international challenges through collaborative legislative action.

His interests included immigration reform, climate change, and healthcare issues. He pushed for the passage of the DREAM Act, which aimed to provide a pathway to citizenship for undocumented immigrants brought to the United States as children. He advocated for sustainable energy policies and healthcare reform. Despite his relatively short tenure in the US Senate, Obama compiled a distinctive legislative record and became known for his ability to work across the aisle to accomplish mutual understanding. He laid the foundation for his signature Hope and Change mantra in his calls for change and unity during his presidential campaign. In the Senate, he honed his legislative skills, expanded his reputation nationally, and developed the policy interests that would later define his presidency.

He captured the attention of influential thought leaders like Warren Buffett, the highly success billionaire investor. The author recalls a time before he announced his candidacy for president, seeing Obama and Buffett hurry through a private club to a back room where the two could meet without interruption. His presence drew the attention of the primarily white, upper-class diners who were curious and bemused by Buffett's interest in the relatively unknown Obama at the time.

He announced his candidacy for the presidency in February 2007. His primary opposition was Senator Hillary Clinton, for whom he had gained respect. However, upon winning his party's nomination, he chose Senator Joe Biden as his vice-presidential running mate. The Obama–Biden ticket faced GOP nominee John McCain, who was persuaded to draft Sarah Palin as his running mate to counter Obama's charismatic attraction. The Obama–Biden team took office on January 20, 2009. Obama inherited a significant economic collapse, wars in Iraq and Afghanistan, and the ongoing threat of terrorism. Obama's presidency was notable for the passage of the Affordable Care Act (ACA), his efforts to recover from the Great Recession, and the operation that led to the death of Osama bin Laden. In 2009, he was awarded the Nobel Peace Prize, the fourth US president to receive the award. He was re-elected in 2012, winning over GOP candidate Mitt Romney.

While there have been many presidents who were lawyers, few described themselves as a community organizer. He credits that experience in his life with a greater appreciation for the value of empathy and achieving common ground in addressing complex problems. He believed common ground extended well beyond mutual understanding. He wrote,

> like any value, empathy must be acted upon. When I was a community organizer back in the eighties, I would often challenge neighborhood leaders by asking them where they put their time, energy, and money. Those were the true tests of what we value, I'd tell them, regardless of what we like to tell ourselves.[24]

As a community organizer in Chicago's poorest African American neighborhoods, "he seemed to be offering himself as the very vision of what America should be—a place where race, class and cultural differences mix together to make a republic whole, not to divide it."[25] With his emphasis on grassroots empowerment and coalition-building, Obama exemplifies characteristics inherent in charismatic leadership (SCL).

Obama crafted a public persona that resonated deeply with a wide swath of the American populace. His narrative was one of hope, change, and the relentless pursuit of a more inclusive and equitable society. Obama's rise to prominence hinged on unity over division, hope over fear, and the shared dreams of all Americans. His message transcended traditional political boundaries, appealing to a diverse coalition of voters who saw in him the embodiment of a new, progressive era in American politics.

Obama was known for his cool, intellectual approach to governance, often seen as a professorial figure who favored reason and deliberation over impulsive decision-making. Despite his initial skepticism of politicians, he eventually crafted an authentic political persona through careful impression management, with skills in self-presentation, nonverbal communication, and social interactions. His speeches were filled with soaring rhetoric and an unshakable belief in American ideals, inspired many, and were a cornerstone of his public image. His use of hand gestures to punctuate messages and his riveting eye contact established a connection with his audience and conveyed confidence and honesty.

Obama's presidency and persona were not without controversy and criticism. Some viewed his approach as too detached or overly conciliatory, arguing that he sometimes fell short of the transformative change he had promised. Specifically, Obama admitted, "failure to pass the DREAM Act was a bitter pill to swallow."[26] The Act would permanently protect certain immigrants who came to the United States as children but were vulnerable to deportation. Nevertheless, his years in office were defined by his commitment to civil discourse, unyielding optimism in adversity, and ability to engage with supporters and critics.

Beyond politics, Obama's personal life—his role as a husband to Michelle Obama and a father to their two daughters—further shaped his public image.

His family life, often shared with the public, painted the picture of a relatable, grounded individual, reinforcing his appeal.

Barack Obama fashioned a public persona that was like that of a trailblazer who embodied hope and change. His intellectual rigor, oratorical skills, and commitment to inclusivity and democracy left an indelible mark on the American presidency and the global stage, defining his legacy as a leader who sincerely believed in the promise of America.

Analysis of Obama's socialized charismatic leadership

Like all leaders, socialized charismatics have a "high need for power but counterbalance it with high activity inhibition, low authoritarianism, an internal locus of control, high self-esteem, and low Machivellianism."[27] Obama is altruistic and consistently focused on the collective interests of others. He engages in debate and sees it as a constructive means to a mutually beneficial outcome. He encourages those around him to achieve desired outcomes and influences by empowering them. He believes people should be empowered to control life events, shunning the idea that outcomes rely on external events. He is highly interested in others, demonstrated by his empathy and focus on self-interest.

Key elements of Obama's leadership style reflecting socialized charismatic leadership

Decision-Making Approach
Deliberative and consultative involving gathering extensive information and consideration of alternatives

Communication
Eloquent and persuasive using inspirational rhetoric emphasizing hope, unity, and change

Motivation Methods
Move hearts and minds through vision of positive change and civic engagement, empowerment, and collective effort

Degree of Control
While maintaining oversight, delegate responsibilities, empowering his team to take initiative. Trust experts

Conflict Resolution
Generally conciliatory aimed at finding common ground. Preferred negotiation and diplomacy

Emotional Intelligence
High EQ with an ability to understand and manage his own emotions, High empathy with others

Vision / Goal Setting
Clear and ambitious goals linked to broader visions for the future and the country especially with health care and climate

Adaptability / Flexibility
Adapt to change, remaining open to modifying his approaches when necessary. Pragmatic, open to compromise

Ethical Behavior
Ethical considerations appeared high in his priorities, emphasizing transparency, accountability, and integrity

Relationship Building
Seeks to build alliances both domestically and internationally, remaining respectful and inclusive

Elements of leadership

Figure 2.1 Elements of Obama's Socialized Charismatic style

Obama's tenure as President of the United States was exemplary of SCL in that we observe their behaviors and attempt to attribute the presence of elements of each type of charismatic leadership, personalized or socialized, accordingly (See Figure 2.1). His leadership seamlessly blended rhetorical finesse with a composed and steady style of embracing the possibilities inherent in his inner circle. He believed in solving problems through time-honored institutions. As a change agent, he fostered his vision for progressive reform tempered by pragmatic considerations. His administrative choices valued a diversity of views, characterized by deliberate inclusivity in key appointments that represented America.

Concerning policy, the Obama administration was distinguished by its dedication to expanding inclusivity, advocating for comprehensive healthcare reform, the rights of the LGBTQ community, and the advancement of racial equity—efforts that ensured the enfranchisement of historically marginalized groups in the American sociopolitical discourse. He based his appeal on creating a better future, one in which the country would celebrate his vision for the country, premised on progressive change, seeking to advance the principles of equality, opportunity, and a shared responsibility for the future.

Obama's foreign policy emphasized multilateral diplomacy, striving to realign the United States' role within the global community and to address pervasive challenges such as the existential threat of climate change and the proliferation of nuclear weapons through concerted international efforts and treaty-based solutions—efforts to reduce the American military presence in these countries, shifting from large-scale military interventions to a strategy that emphasized targeted counterterrorism efforts, diplomacy, and multilateral partnerships. This shift was part of a broader strategy to move away from the unilateral military actions of the early 2000s and toward a more sustainable and collaborative approach to international security.

Domestically, the passage and implementation of the Affordable Care Act (ACA), dubbed Obamacare, was a comprehensive healthcare reform legislation that significantly overhauled the US healthcare system. It aimed at reducing the cost of health insurance, expanding access to coverage, and reducing practices deemed by Democrats to be detrimental to consumers, such as denying coverage for pre-existing conditions. While not perfect, the ACA fulfilled a long-standing goal of many Democrats: to move the United States closer to universal healthcare coverage. Facing substantial political opposition and legal challenges, including a challenge in the Supreme Court, resulted in millions of previously uninsured Americans gaining health insurance.

The Obama presidency bespoke the SCL approach in how it advocated for progressive policy changes. Opposition fomented rapidly in the perception of America's role in international relations. As opposed to pressing on, Obama's administration advocated a vigorous discourse on American national identity while re-assessing its stance on the global scene.

Impression management skills are an earmark of charismatic leaders. Closely monitoring public perception plays a significant role in garnering the support and trust of followers. Figure 2.2 demonstrates how Obama's followers resonated with his message. His ability to control and manage the impressions he made on others was evident in several key areas:

- Communication: An accomplished orator, Obama effectively conveyed messages convincingly, shaping public perception. He was relatable while inspiring confidence and trust, which contributed to the authority granted by his followers.
- Public Image: As mentioned, being dubbed "No Drama Obama" is evidence that people were comforted by his steady leadership.
- Relatability: A gifted storyteller, he shared experiences that made him approachable and relatable. He openly talked about his family life and personal challenges that contributed to his eventual successes. In the vernacular, he was the kind of guy you'd like to have a beer with, even if you disagreed with him.
- Handling Controversy: Obama addressed issues directly, calmly, and reasonably as a consummate manager of impressions that diminished negative

Obama's values reflected in a recognizable motif representing hope and change

Obama campaign rally in Fort Worth, Tx on February 28, 2008. Photo Credit: Charles Ommanney

Figure 2.2 Followers celebrating their devotion to the Obama brand

perceptions. He maintained his priority to talk things out and arrive at mutual understanding.
- Consistency: Obama's underlying themes of hope, change, and inclusivity established a fresh approach to relations, creating a positive identity in the public's mind, and reinforcing his credibility and trustworthiness.
- Cultural Competence: His command of cultural distinctions connected with diverse groups who often felt alienated. He demonstrated empathy through his understanding of varied American experiences.

As evidenced in Figure 2.2, Obama's followers enthusiastically bought into his message of hope. He effectively communicated, maintaining a positive public image that related to a broad audience. This transparency in communication equipped him to handle controversies with poise while remaining consistent in his values and identity. These were vital factors in shaping public perception and facilitating his leadership role on the national and global stage.

His relationship with religious communities and impact on these groups caused him to think of "himself as a Christian who prays regularly and seeks religious guidance for the actions he takes as a leader and in his personal life" [xxviii]. True to his demeanor, Obama protected his faith life from public view. He adopted the Trinity United Church of Christ and practiced full-throated expression of religious beliefs. The contrast, along with Obama's varying level of alignment with spiritual issues (e.g., abortion, government providing contraceptives), presented inherent conflict that could erupt [xxix].

Throughout his tenure, Obama sought to bridge gaps between diverse faith communities. He demonstrated even-handedness, open dialogue, and mutual respect while extending outreach to Christians, Muslims, Jews, Hindus, Sikhs, and non-believers. This approach fostered a climate of inclusivity and understanding across religious lines.

His appreciation for diversity influenced Obama's engagement with religious communities. He often spoke of his faith's role in motivating social justice and its importance in public life, evidenced by his administration's outreach to various faith groups, including Christian denominations Jewish, Muslim, Buddhist, and Hindu communities. From his early days as a community organizer, Obama knew the organizing value of religious groups. For example, he observed the benefit of the way Saul Alinsky's Industrial Areas Foundation (IAF) connected with "the liberal wing of the Catholic Church, whose parishes served as sponsoring members of local organizations . . . [providing community] . . . leadership from the ranks of laypeople, nuns, and priests and paid dues to keep the apparatus going" [xxx],

His support for abortion rights and same-sex marriage ran headlong into conflict with the teachings of many conservative religious groups, leading to criticism and opposition. His healthcare mandate requiring employers to provide contraception coverage drew the ire of the Catholic Church and other religious organizations that opposed contraception on religious grounds. Despite this, Obama sought to bridge divides and find common ground. He emphasized the shared values of different faith traditions, such as caring for the less fortunate and the moral imperative of justice and equality. His speeches often included scriptural references, drawing from various religious traditions to underscore his points about unity and compassion. He was open about his faith and avowed how it guided his life and decisions. He regularly attended church services and participated in prayer breakfasts, using these occasions to discuss his spiritual beliefs and the role of faith in guiding the nation's conscience.

If there is a recurring theme in Barack Obama's public persona regarding religion, it might be fiery rhetoric. The controversy surrounding Obama and his former pastor, Jeremiah Wright, threatened to overshadow Obama's presidential campaign, challenging his message of unity and hope. This narrative began in the heart of Chicago, where Obama's spiritual journey intersected with Wright's fiery rhetoric. Wright is a pastor known for his passionate sermons and outspoken views. He served as the pastor of Trinity United Church of Christ in Chicago, where Barack Obama and his family attended church for many years. Wright played a significant role in Obama's spiritual life, even inspiring the title of Obama's book, *The Audacity of Hope*. However, controversy erupted on the national stage.

In the heat of the 2008 presidential campaign, video clips of Wright's sermons began circulating in the media. In these clips, Wright made inflammatory remarks, criticizing the United States government and society at large for its policies and history of racial inequality. On March 13, ABC News released a composite of Wright's clips on a Good Morning America broadcast segment. While Wright's grievances resonated with his followers on Sunday morning, they alarmed the predominantly white, secular morning TV audience. In one clip, Wright profanely pronounced, "Not God bless America, God damn America." This inflammatory rhetoric contradicted Obama's message of reconciliation and optimism. The media amplified public outcry that was damaging to Obama's reputation.

Critics questioned how Obama could reconcile his campaign's unifying message with his long-standing association with Wright, whose comments were not just sensational but seen as divisive and unpatriotic. The controversy grew to proportions that threatened to derail Obama's candidacy, forcing him to confront the issue head-on—a quintessential SCL-styled response. Obama faulted himself for

> the pure hubris that led him to believe he could dip in and out of a complex institution like Trinity headed by a complex man like Reverend Wright and select as if off a menu, only those things that I liked. Maybe I could do that as a private citizen, but not as a public figure.[28]

Obama's presidency was characterized by a conscious and multifaceted engagement with the diverse spectrum of religious communities, a testament to his faith journey and the varied fabric of American religious life. This relationship was consciously formed reflecting his transformative spiritual experience, which began in a secular home life through adolescence and culminated in his adult commitment to Christianity within the congregation of Trinity United Church of Christ in Chicago. This personal evolution underpinned his approach to faith in public life—a commitment deeply informed by his private devotion balanced by his mindful distinction between personal belief and public duty.

This chapter provided a backdrop blending scholarly evidence characterizing the well-studied phenomenon of charismatic leadership with a narrative chronicling the relevant elements of Barack Obama's life and career, particularly as it pertains to highlighting his brand of SCL. Obama's leadership style combines inspirational and charismatic elements with a consensus-building, analytical, and pragmatic approach. He was noted for his composed demeanor, progressive yet pragmatic policies, commitment to diversity and inclusion, and a strong orientation toward international diplomacy and cooperation.

Notes

1 Maraniss, D. (2012). *Barack Obama: The story*. New York, NY: Simon & Schuster, p. 265.
2 Ibid, (pp. 265–266).
3 Ibid, (p. 266).
4 Ibid, (p. 301).
5 Ibid.
6 Obama, B. (2020). *A promised land*. New York, NY: Crown Books, p. 6.
7 Ibid.
8 Ibid, (p. 112).
9 Ibid, (p. 113).
10 Mendell, (p. 34).
11 Maraniss (2012), (p. xix).
12 Ibid.
13 Ibid, (p. xxi).
14 Ibid, (p. 10).
15 Ibid.
16 Ibid, (p. 11).
17 Obama (2020), (p. 12).
18 Maraniss (2012), (p. 32).
19 Ibid.
20 Ibid, (p. 33).
21 Ibid.
22 Obama, B. (2006). *The audacity of hope*. New York, NY: Crown Books, p. 2.
23 https://www.google.com/search?client=firefox-b-1-d&q=what+was+obama%27s+margin+of+victory+n+the+2004+illinois+us+senate+race.
24 Obama (2006), (p. 67).
25 Ibid, (p. 66).

26 Obama (2020), (p. 619).
27 Conger, J. A., and Kanungo, R. N. (1998). *Charismatic leadership in organizations*. Thousand Oaks, CA: SAGE, p. 212.
28 Ibid, (p. 141).

Reference List

Conger, J. A., and Kanungo, R. N. (1998). *Charismatic leadership in organizations*. Thousand Oaks, CA: SAGE.

Maraniss, D. (2012). *Barack Obama: The story*. New York, NY: Simon & Schuster.

McKenzie, B.D. McKenzie, Brian D., '"It's Complicated": The Obama Administration's Relationship with Black Faith Communities and Lessons for Future Presidents', in Todd Shaw, Robert A. Brown, and Joseph P. McCormick (eds), *After Obama: African American Politics in a Post-Obama Era* (New York, NY, 2021; online edn, NYU Press Scholarship Online, 23 Sept. 2021), https://doi.org/10.18574/nyu/9781479807277.003.0005, accessed 18 July 2024.

Mendell, D. (2008). *Obama: From promise to power*. New York, NY: Amistad.

Miller, L. (2008, July 11). Q&A: What Barack Obama prays for. *Newsweek*.

Obama, B. (2006). *The audacity of hope*. New York, NY: Crown Books.

Obama, B. (2020). *A promised land*. New York, NY: Crown Books.

3 Donald Trump's charismatic leadership

Background and rise to prominence

Donald Trump, the 45th president of the United States, was born on June 14, 1946, in the Queens borough of New York City. He is an American businessman, television personality, and politician. Trump is known for being the first US president without prior military or government service.

Trump was raised in a wealthy family, the fourth of five children of Fred Trump, a real estate developer, and Mary Anne MacLeod Trump. He attended the New York Military Academy and, in 1968, received a bachelor's degree in economics from the Wharton School of the University of Pennsylvania. After graduating, Trump joined his family's real estate business in New York City. In 1971, he took control of the company and renamed it "The Trump Organization." He expanded the business operations from Queens and Brooklyn into Manhattan, developing and constructing office towers, hotels, casinos, and golf courses. Trump also branded and managed numerous properties with his name, establishing his reputation in the real estate industry.

In the opening pages of his best-selling book, *The Art of the Deal*, Trump succinctly summarizes his work ethic:

> Most people are surprised by the way I work. I play it very loose. I don't carry a briefcase. I try not to schedule too many meetings. I leave my door open. You can't be imaginative or entrepreneurial if you've got too much structure. I prefer to come to work each day and just see what develops.[1]

Trump presented himself as a high-level businessman who defied conventional behavior. He was the quintessential populist who championed various popular views that juxtaposed the common people with the elites. According to journalist Maggie Haberman (2022), "Trump was notorious for seeking cues that would help him please his audience,"[2] often asking interviewers what they wanted him to say, ostensibly to help them craft a favorable story of him. He was acutely aware that messaging was part of his plan to perform on a bigger stage.

DOI: 10.4324/9781003463047-4

Trump was a staple of the New York City tabloids, earning a reputation for success in projecting an endearing mix of flamboyance and toughness. Establishing his brand at an early age gained him popularity in the New York City area and the real estate industry. Still, it was not until he appeared as the host of *The Apprentice* that he gained national fame as a celebrity. Following his success with *Survivor*, an unscripted reality TV show, Mark Burnett cast Trump as a benevolent billionaire, reviewing the individual performances of a rotating cast of stage and screen stars, tycoons, impresarios, artists, performers, and musicians in competition for a management job in The Trump Organization.

Like *Survivor*, one of the contestants was dismissed each week based on their performance of a business task devised by and judged by Trump, their dismissal punctuated by the terse phrase, "You're fired!" The show became a rating sensation, significantly expanding Trump's image nationally as a successful and outspoken businessman and authority figure. A significant nuance in each production rested in Trump's insistence that all participants address him by "Sir" or the honorific "Mister," elevating him to a position of respect. Though subtle, through repetitive and consistent use—a treatment Trump knew used effectively—this imbued him with status in viewers' eyes, numbering six-to-seven million an episode.

Raised by a strong, authoritative, and resolute father prepared Donald Trump to present a confident public stance, undaunted in his quest for his dream. "He ultimately fulfilled his father's desire for a successor in the family business: real estate. But what the son really always wanted was to be a star."[3] Trump was indeed his father's pre-ordained choice. In his early years, he enjoyed an enviable childhood in a fashionable section of Queens. He was considered impulsive, mischievous, and intimidating when the situation warranted. His home life was replete with maids and chauffeurs to meet the family's needs. It was made possible by his father's success in real estate, a field of endeavor the senior Trump saw fit to determine would be Donald's career path from an early age.

This life of privilege was suddenly interrupted when Trump was in 7th grade. His father, Fred, found some knives in Donald's room that he had with a neighborhood friend on a "trip to the jungle," specifically Times Square, a seedy place at the time. The elder Trump was not one to equivocate in word or deed. Fred Trump saw a need for course correction in the form of discipline and immediately dispatched young Donald to the New York Military Academy (NYMA)[4] in Cornwall, New York. It was a move to "introduce discipline to a boy who was headstrong,"[5] The Trumps "could have chosen any private school, but chose a military academy so that they could neutralize the richness of his upbringing and knock some discipline into him."[6] Young Donald finished his secondary education there and then attended Fordham University for two years before transferring to Wharton School, where he completed his undergraduate schooling. Trump "had already started taking on deals by the time he was at

Wharton. That was what interested him more than anything else. He wanted to do deals, and he wanted to make money."[7]

Upon graduation, Trump understood that his father needed a successor, a decision the elder Trump had not yet made known. He preferred his namesake, Fred Jr.; however, Freddie was easygoing and friendly and did not reflect the fierce nature preferred by his father. Eventually, much to his father's and younger brother's disdain, Fred Jr. left the business and became a commercial pilot. Tragically, as a direct result of his abuse of alcohol, Freddie died at the age of 42. "Donald would cite for decades as the reason why—for all his excesses—he abstained from alcohol. 'I watched him,' Trump later told a reporter of his brother's fall, 'and I learned from him.'"[8]

When he entered the New York scene in the early 1970s, Trump lived a fast-paced lifestyle and fostered a "playboy" image. He frequented the trendy hot spots Manhattan had to offer, including Le Club, a members-only restaurant, and nightclub in midtown Manhattan. There, he met Roy Cohn, a lawyer who gained fame as Senator Joseph McCarthy's chief counsel during the Army-McCarthy hearings in 1954, which investigated suspected communists operating in America. In that meeting, he told Cohn he abhorred lawyers because "I think all they do is delay deals, instead of making deals, and every answer they give you is no, and they are always looking to settle instead of fight."[9] Cohn agreed.

Trump then pleaded his case, where he believed the government unjustly charged The Trump Organization with rent discrimination.[10] According to Trump, after hearing his account, Cohn responded, "I don't think you have any obligation to rent to tenants who would be undesirable, white or black, and the government doesn't have the right to run your business."[11] Cohn's retaliatory response delighted Trump, and he hired Cohn to take the case. The suit was eventually settled, finding that the Trump organization was culpable of the charges with the stipulation there would be no public admission of guilt. Cohn was one of many lawyers Trump has deployed to represent him as a plaintiff or defendant throughout his career.

Trump and his business entities have been involved in many lawsuits, reflecting the vast scope and scale of his business operations and his aggressive stance with adversaries. From the 1970s until he was elected president in 2016, Donald Trump and his businesses were involved in 4,095 legal cases in United States federal and state courts, including 85 branding and trademark cases, 17 campaign cases, 1,863 casino cases, 208 contract dispute cases, 130 employment cases, 63 golf club cases, 190 government and tax cases, 14 media or defamation cases, 609 personal injury cases, 622 real estate cases, 99 miscellaneous cases, and 206 other cases.[12]

Trump's business success, primarily in investments, spans various sectors, including real estate, luxury hotels, golf courses, and residential properties. His holdings include iconic properties like Trump Tower in New York City and Mar-a-Lago in Florida, as well as a range of other properties across the

United States and in international locations such as Scotland and Ireland. He has dealt extensively in licensing his name and brand for a range of products and services, including clothing lines, home furnishings, and even steaks. This branding strategy has been a lucrative source of income and has expanded his investment reach beyond direct real estate holdings.

He has also invested in media, particularly television, and, more recently, Truth Social,[13] a social media platform, and in stocks and other financial instruments. Over the years, Trump has ventured into a wide range of businesses, including airlines (Trump Shuttle), beauty pageants (Miss Universe), and educational ventures (Trump University). During his 2024 presidential campaign, Trump introduced official gold-colored Trump presidential sneakers at $400 each and a "God Bless the USA" bible for $59.99 each.

In 2011, Trump seized on challenging Obama's country of birth, claiming the president was not born in the United States. Known as the "Birther Movement"—it was premised on a baseless claim that takes on a life of its own. Akin to a rumor, it spreads without a quick, direct, and logical explanation, challenging its credibility. While the media readily reported on this spurious conspiracy theory, and even though the White House produced evidence of the birth certificate, "birthers" argued it was not genuine and, therefore, there is no proof Obama was born in the United States, thus disqualifying Obama to hold office. It was a trial balloon for Trump, a successful foray into an alternate reality, a test he effectively learned such charges of corrupt behavior needed little evidence to impact public opinion significantly. It was a harbinger of things to come.

As a politician, he switched between the Republican, Democratic, Independent, and special-interest parties over the years. In 2000, he tested the political environment by running for the Reform Party's presidential nomination but withdrew before the voting began. In the years following, Trump consistently expressed interest in running for president in various interviews and speeches. At one point in 2011, a *Wall Street Journal/NBC News* poll showed Trump leading all presidential contenders, including Mitt Romney, the eventual Republican Party nominee.[14] By the time he had descended the gold and marble ensconced escalator at Trump Tower in 2015, he had honed his persona to reflect a robust, able-bodied champion prepared to take the people's grievances to the ballot box. To the uninitiated, Trump broke all the rules of successful image-making, while to "his people," he was the savior they were awaiting. His relentless rejection of what was considered politically correct was the catalyst for casting himself as a champion of truth, not truth itself, a lesson he learned in his unabashed public exploits.

In her extensive biography of Trump, Maggie Haberman wrote of his unique take on power: "Other than his father, the most important influence on the future president was Roy Cohn, who taught him how to construct an entire life around proximity to power, avoiding responsibility and creating artifice through media."[15] This morphed into a quasi-authoritarian stance, where power is recognized by combining the leader's and the public's attribution of an authoritarian mentality or attitude. Trump aides said early in his presidency, Trump likened his power to that of the "once-powerful Democratic Party machines in those [New York] boroughs where a single boss controlled everything in his kingdom. And knew his support alone could ensure electoral success."[16] For Trump, the adoption of this concept was a natural outgrowth of growing up surrounded by confident men who saw incertitude as weakness. As has been witnessed, Trump never backs down; he doubles down.

Donald Trump's rise to the presidency coincided with a significant shift in American politics. It highlighted deep national divisions and sparked intense political and social debates. Trump fronted bold, populist views that attracted disassociated voters. Many of these citizens were not active in elections, but when Trump gave their cause a voice, they went to the polls in droves, particularly in small towns and rural America. Trump's self-aggrandizing style was no more evident than in 2016 when he took the stage at the Republican National Convention as the party's newly anointed presidential choice. *The Atlantic* aptly captured a display of his almighty hubris:

> *I am your voice*, said Trump. *I alone can fix it. I will restore law and order.* He did not appeal to prayer or God. He did not ask Americans to measure him against their values or to hold him responsible for living up to them. He did not ask for their help. He asked them to place their faith in him.[17]

This kind of rhetoric is bold and focused on the speaker's abilities, albeit in a hyperbolic context. Trump's proclamation was premised on and stimulated by followers' unrelenting adulation and growing loyalty. It is highly effective messaging because it is clear and direct. It is an example of his acumen in the art of impression management. From the receiver's perspective—Trump's followers—it struck a chord of discontent in a core group of citizens who felt they had been left behind. With Trump, they found someone with whom they could identify, with whom they could instill trust, and with whom they felt compelled to commit an uncommon level of loyalty.

Overview of Trump's leadership skills, style, and public persona

Trump launched his campaign for president on June 16, 2015, in a brash and attention-getting manner that was directly aimed at his target audience, a segment of the population who felt they had no voice in their government. He focused on issues such as immigration reform by proclaiming the need for a wall to be built along the US–Mexico border, repeal of the Obama-era Affordable Care Act, and promoting American manufacturing, repudiating international trade with China as nothing more than exporting jobs abroad, especially to China. His position on these topics was expressed in opposition to the status quo and, more pointedly, as a means to undermine accomplishments claimed by the Obama Administration.

As is the hallmark of charismatic leaders, it is not only the discrepant message but also the forceful way it is delivered that matters. Consider Trump's shocking message that shakes the foundation of the status quo:

> When Mexico sends its people, they're not sending their best. They're not sending you, [he repeats] they're not sending you (points to the assembled crowd), they are sending people who have lots of problems, and they are bringing those problems with us [*sic*]. They are bringing drugs, they are bringing crime, they are rapists . . . and some, I assume, are good people. But I speak to border guards, and they tell us that's not what we're getting . . . [then he delivers the solution]. We need a leader who can bring back our jobs, can bring back our manufacturing, can bring back our military, can take care of our vets, our vets have been abandoned.[18]

Brazenly, he delivered the opening salvo of his campaign in Trump trademark fashion, complete with his distinctive, no-holds-barred style of speech, strident assertiveness, and uncanny ability to connect with a segment of the population that was long overdue to hear a leader who is not a politician deliver a glancing blow at the bureaucracy. The charismatic leader knows the bounds of messaging and pushes them to the limit.

His direct and assertive approach marks Donald Trump's leadership style. He evokes strength, decisiveness, and authority. He relies on his instinct in decision-making, preferring to render a quickly generated opinion rather than deliberating or consulting with others. When communicating, he is straightforward and unfiltered. In a press conference with Homeland Security's science and technology team at the height of the pandemic, Trump spontaneously reacted to a statement made by an official to eradicate the virus:

> I see the disinfectant . . . knocks it out in a minute, one minute . . . is there a way we can do something like that by injection inside or almost a cleaning? As you see, it [the virus] gets in the lungs, it does a tremendous number on the lungs, so it would be interesting to check that.[19]

This retort is an example of Trump speaking off-the-cuff in his role as a self-perceived problem-solver or idea generator. This out-of-the-box thinking, as novel ideation is often called, is a valued asset in brainstorming sessions; however, as a statement from an authority figure in a live, public news conference, it portrays the speaker as reckless, even thoughtless, especially in his role as president at the time. NBC reported,

> Medical professionals, including Dr. Vin Gupta, a pulmonologist and global health policy expert . . . were quick to challenge the president's "improper

health messaging. . . . This notion of injecting or ingesting any type of cleansing product into the body is irresponsible, and it's dangerous," said Gupta. "It's a common method that people utilize when they want to kill themselves."

As a leader who is ever vigilant in defending his reputation at any hint of challenge, Trump viewed cautionary statements like Gupta's as criticism of him, something he would not tolerate. In the same press conference, Trump seized on a fact he heard from one of the experts, who said that direct sunlight killed the coronavirus pathogen. Trump suggested light might be inserted into the body and that would serve as a clever means of elimination. Relentless, his comments revealed a side of Trump as a creative problem-solver, albeit clever to the point of being absurd. Yet experienced creative thinkers will suggest practical ideas that often stem from seemingly preposterous suggestions. One might ask, is he a savant or a lunatic? The answer is in the eye of the beholder. This imaginative conjecture stymies the unimpressed observer while enrapturing his loyal fans. This day-to-day autocratic drama clearly showed that Trump exemplifies characteristics inherent in PCL.

Key elements of Trump's leadership style
Reflecting personalized charismatic leadership

Decision-Making Approach
Intuitive and unilateral relying on personal beliefs and instincts rather than analysis or consultation with others

Communication
Direct, assertive, controversial. Preference in using social media bypassing traditional media

Motivation Methods
Assertive, provocative rhetoric to mobilize his base of loyal supporters through definitive, inspirational messages

Degree of Control
High level of control with centralized decision-making. A tight grip on the narrative and his team. Question experts

Conflict Resolution
Confrontational, publicly challenging opponents and critics through direct attacks and raw language

Emotional Intelligence
He connects and energizes supporters but lacks genuine empathy and consideration of differing perspectives

Vision / Goal Setting
Clear and straightforward centered on nationalistic and protectionist themes. Bold and ambitious

Adaptability / Flexibility
A mix of rigidity in core beliefs, yet tactical flexibility shifting positions based on the situation or public opinion

Ethical Behavior
Supporters see him as true to his beliefs, challenging the status quo. Critics question is adherence to ethical norms

Relationship Building
Places high value on loyalty and allegiance to him, yet quick to cut off relationship to those who disagree with him

Conger & Kanungo, 1998 **SOURCE: Adapted from Conger (1990, p. 52)**

Figure 3.1 A synopsis of Trump's personalized charismatic style

These incidents may explain why Trump preferred communicating directly to the public through social media channels, like Twitter/X, bypassing direct communication with the news media. His aversion to reporters was so strong that he referred to the national press corps as an enemy of the people. On April 5, 2019, *The Hill*, the largest politically significant site in the United States, reported, "President Trump said Friday that the press is 'truly the enemy of the people,' ratcheting up his use of the derisive label to attack the news media."[20]

Trump frequently used the press and its reporting as a foil, drawing attention to his successes. By identifying a critic, he could call them out as an organized attempt to prevent his good work from happening, for example, "The press is doing everything within their power to fight the magnificence of the phrase, MAKE AMERICA GREAT AGAIN!" Trump tweeted.[21] Trump understood by employing Twitter to launch his opinions, ideas, and insults, his loyal followers would rapidly multiply his message by re-distributing it to millions through their Re-Tweets, a simple means of sending the message to their followers. Further, by taking an active role in advancing the message, Trump loyalists were exhibiting transference, a psychological term meaning the act of advancing Trump's message. Followers were subconsciously projecting the feelings, desires, and fantasies of Trump onto themselves and others.

While he demands loyalty, he discourages questioning his judgment and punishes those who oppose him. Several vital characteristics underscore this style and define Trump's method of governance and influence. Trump's direct and assertive communication, especially using social media platforms such as Twitter, symbolizes his personalized approach. He bypassed traditional media outlets to communicate directly with the public, establishing an unmediated channel for his narrative and messaging. This method affords him the space to set the agenda and maintain a constant presence in the public discourse.

Analysis of Trump's personalized charismatic approach

The distinguishing factors that apply to personalized charismatics are a "high need for power [that unlike socialized leaders] is coupled with low activity inhibition, high authoritarianism, an external locus of control, low self-esteem, high narcissism, and high Machiavellianism." Trump is egotistic and focused primarily on the intent to benefit self. Trump prefers to rely on his instincts in decision-making and rarely seeks alternate opinions. In this manner, he demonstrates a preference to govern in a totalitarian style, with a high disregard for established institutional channels. He expects his inner circle to be obedient. Trump employs empathy to understand the feelings of others and craft a message that will ring true, serving his purpose of serving his personal needs.

Trump's tenure as president of the United States was exemplary of PCL in that we observe his behaviors and attempt to attribute the presence of elements of each type of charismatic leadership, personalized or socialized, accordingly. His leadership demonstrated an authoritative and decisive nature, often bordering on autocratic. Trump's tendency to make swift and usually binary decisions underscored his self-portrayal as a strong leader with an apparent gift for problem-solving. He considered bureaucracy an obstacle and sought to subvert it at all costs. This decisiveness was integral to his appeal among supporters who desired definitive action and perceived him as capable of effectuating change.

Embracing populism over policy, Trump positioned himself as the voice of the common man, rallying against the established political, economic, and cultural elites. This approach tapped into the sentiments of individuals who felt overlooked by the political system and resonated with voters' discontent with the status quo. He based his appeal on change, specifically to return to a better time enjoyed in the past. Trump's vision for the country was characterized by a populist "America First" approach, emphasizing economic growth, national security, and a strong national identity while pushing back against globalization, liberal immigration policies, and multilateral international agreements.

Trump's foreign policy underscored his skepticism of multilateralism and preference for bilateral negotiations, which was also evident in his demands for increased cost-sharing by allies in military alliances such as NATO. Trump's foreign policy was marked by the belief that previous administrations had allowed other nations to exploit the United States economically and militarily, and rectifying this was his primary foreign policy objective.

Domestically, Trump sought to address the fears he witnessed in the zeitgeist of the day, generally centered on a feeling by many that the country is on the wrong course. This fear reflects a combination of skepticism, demand for reform, and partisanship. Trust in the federal government remains near record lows, with fewer than two in ten Americans expressing that they trust the government to do what is right "just about always" or "most of the time."[22] There is a noticeable division between Democrats and Republicans on this question, with 25% of Democrats and only 8% of Republicans currently reporting trust in the federal government.[23] Figure 3.2 captures the emotional relationship that Trump brought about by giving voice to simmering fears.

Hot-button issues included immigration reform, economic policy (emphasis on nationalism), foreign policy (isolationist), and energy independence (reliance on domestic supplies). Trump's transactional and results-oriented mindset, stemming from his business background, influenced his approach to governance. He viewed political interactions through the lens of deal-making, prioritizing negotiations that would yield visible results. This focus on measurable outcomes was frequently spotlighted in his emphasis on economic achievements and his negotiation of trade deals.

Messiah or Guardian? Trump's followers visibly bestow the gift of charisma

Trump Rally in Mobile, AL, August 21, 2015 **=Photo Credit: Mark Wallheiser**

Figure 3.2 Followers celebrating their devotion to Trump and his brand

Trump is well practiced at impression management skills, a core component of his public persona, which can be summarized as follows:

- Communication: Trump's direct and unfiltered communication style, particularly on social media channels like Twitter/X, and, later on, Truth Social, has had a profound impact on his base. His straightforward, simple language resonates with them, keeping him at the forefront of the public conversation and making his words a powerful, influencing force.
- Public Image: His public image is that of a brash and bold outsider, a business mogul unafraid to challenge political norms. Trump carefully cultivated this image of a non-establishment figure who speaks his mind, which appealed to voters skeptical of traditional politics.
- Reliability: Opinions are divided on his reliability. His supporters view him as consistent in his commitment to his promises on the campaign trail, particularly regarding issues like immigration and trade. Critics point to factual inaccuracies and shifting positions undermining his reliability among the general public.
- Handling Controversy: Trump has a distinctive approach to controversy, often engaging directly and combatively. He tends to double down on his

positions and uses controversy to dominate media narratives and rally his base rather than retreat or seek reconciliation, a course heretofore to be the proper way to handle such matters.
- Consistency: While Trump has consistently promoted specific key themes and issues, such as Make America Great Again, his policy positions have sometimes been fluid, bending with the shifting public opinion. Depending on one's perspective, this adaptability can be seen as a strategic advantage or a lack of foundational principles.
- Cultural Competence: Trump's cultural competence—his ability to effectively recognize and navigate the values of different cultural groups—is often debated. He has a strong connection with his core constituency, which often feels overlooked by mainstream culture, but he has also been criticized for insensitivity and divisiveness regarding multiculturalism and international relations.

In summary, his ability to effectively shape his persona and value as a leader is well served by his skills and approaches to impression management, which have significantly shaped Trump's political career and unique position in American public life.

Relationship with religious communities and impact on these groups

Donald Trump's relationship with religious groups, particularly evangelical Christians, has been one of the more intriguing dynamics of his political career. Despite a personal history that seemed at odds with the traditional values espoused by many religious conservatives, Trump managed to forge a strong alliance with this cohort, underscoring the complex nature of political and religious alliances. Recognizing his vulnerability, the choice of his vice president, Mike Pence, was calculated to establish a connection and build credibility with a constituency considered to be at odds with Trump's life choices. It was a fruitful decision.

Trump's flair for living a gregarious lifestyle, replete locker-room talk about the misogynistic treatment of women,[24] a history of multiple marriages, and a reputation for a lavish lifestyle initially appeared to be an unlikely pedigree of a champion for evangelical and conservative religious voters. However, as he campaigned for and assumed the presidency, he adeptly shifted the criteria to his equally well-honed reputation as a staunch defender of religious freedoms and conservative values, winning over many in these communities.

Trump fostered a pragmatic and symbiotic relationship with religious communities, particularly evangelical Christians and conservative faith-based groups. This relationship had profound implications for his administration's policies and the political landscape of religious America. At the core of Trump's engagement with religious constituencies was a strategic alignment with evangelical Christians. He appealed to their core concerns by vocally opposing abortion, advocating for religious education, and nominating them to the federal bench. These actions cemented his support among these groups, who, in turn, he came to rely on them to support his political agenda.

In policy terms, Trump's administration took tangible steps that aligned with the priorities of religious groups. Notably, he recognized Jerusalem as Israel's capital and relocated the US Embassy there, a move lauded by many evangelical Christians and conservative Jewish communities. This decision represented his commitment to fulfilling essential campaign promises to his religious supporters. Trump advanced the perception of his dedication to these groups through his high visibility at public appearances at events like the March for Life, his speeches extolling religious freedom, and his administration's actions to protect the rights of religious organizations in healthcare, education, and other areas. He portrayed himself as a protector of religious liberty and was often framed by his supporters as a bulwark against secularism and liberal policies perceived to threaten religious values.

However, Trump's presidency was not without controversies, especially regarding his rhetoric and policy positions that divided public opinion. His hardline approach to immigration and comments on Islam elicited significant backlash from various religious communities and leaders, reflecting the divisive nature of his political and cultural impact. His executive order early in his presidency banning travel to the United States from seven Muslim-majority countries drew the ire of religious leaders, including Bishop Joe S. Vásquez of the US Conference of Catholic Bishops, "We need to protect all our brothers and sisters of all faiths, including Muslims, who have lost family, home and country."[25] The issue was challenged in the courts, where the Supreme Court ruled in favor of Trump's right to invoke the ban but reserved opinion on the soundness of the decision.

Trump met with Evangelicals behind closed doors at an invitation-only meeting in the summer before the 2016 election to settle their concerns about his behavior and stance on issues affecting Christians, including litigation on religious rights, precisely issues around "same-sex weddings, restrictions on prayer in public schools, and a growing move to allow transgender people to use the bathrooms they choose."[26] According to a reporter at the meeting, Trump effectively addressed their concerns and certified his promise to remove the governmental encumbrances on religious freedom.

Trump exerted substantial cultural influence. His presidency empowered a segment of religious America that felt overshadowed by progressive cultural trends. His presidency reinvigorated their public discourse on the role of religion in society and politics, leading to a more vocal presence of conservative religious viewpoints in the national conversation, reviving the term "culture war" in the American conversation, a term meaning a conflict between the values of progressives and traditionalists dating back 100 years.[27] Trump's administration was noted for its close engagement with religious leaders who supported his policies. These leaders were provided significant access to the

White House, influencing policy decisions and enjoying a level of visibility uncommon in previous administrations.

Donald Trump's relationship with religious groups, particularly evangelical Christians, has been one of the more intriguing dynamics of his political career. Despite a personal history that seemed at odds with the traditional values espoused by many religious conservatives, Trump managed to forge a strong alliance with this cohort, underscoring the complex nature of political and religious alliances.

Trump's appointments of conservative judges to the federal judiciary, including the Supreme Court, were seen as victories for those hoping to influence rulings on abortion, religious freedom, and other key issues. His administration's strong stance in favor of Israel, including moving the US Embassy to Jerusalem, resonated deeply with evangelical Christians who view the support of Israel as a biblical mandate.

Despite criticisms and skepticism about the authenticity of his religious convictions, Trump maintained a strong base of support among evangelical and conservative religious voters throughout his presidency. This relationship was characterized by a pragmatic alliance, where the mutual benefits of policy achievements and political support countered personal misgivings about his character or past behaviors.

Donald Trump's relationship with religious groups, particularly evangelical Christians, was marked by a strategic alignment of interests. Despite a personal life that contrasted with the moral and ethical standards typically upheld by these groups, his policy decisions and public stance on crucial issues effectively cultivated and maintained their support, illustrating the often pragmatic nature of political and religious alliances.

Notes

1 Trump, D. J., and Schwartz, T. (1987). *The art of the deal*. New York, NY: Ballantine Books, p. 1.
2 Haberman, M. (2022). *Confidence man: The making of Donald Trump and the breaking of America*. New York, NY: Penguin Press, p. 1.
3 Ibid, (p. 2).
4 The New York Military Academy attracted students of note, including Art Davies, founder of the Ultimate Fighting Championship, mobster John Gotti, and composer Charles Sondheim, to name a few.
5 MacGregor, J. R. (2019). *Trump the biography*. Sheridan, WY: CAC Publishing LLC, p. 105.
6 Ibid.
7 Ibid, (p. 131).
8 Haberman (2022), (p. 29).
9 Trump and Schwartz (1987), (p. 96).
10 This case originated in 1972 when two individuals posing as would-be renters posing undercover as "testers" for a government-sanctioned investigation to determine if Trump Management Inc. discriminated against minorities seeking housing at properties across Brooklyn and Queens. https://www.

washingtonpost.com/politics/inside-the-governments-racial-bias-case-against-donald-trumps-company-and-how-he-fought-it/2016/01/23/fb90163e-bfbe-11e5-bcda-62a36b394160_story.html.

11 Ibid, (p. 98).

12 This information was obtained from an article in *USA Today* titled "Donald Trump: Three decades 4.095 lawsuits." https://www.usatoday.com/pages/interactives/trump-lawsuits/

13 On April 1, 2024, according to CNN, Trump Media & Technology Group, the owner of struggling social media platform Truth Social, began its long-delayed journey as a public company at Tuesday's opening bell under the ticker symbol "DJT." The Associated Press (04/04/24) reported DJT shares traded at $48.00/share a week after a high of $79.00/share. https://fortune.com/author/associated-press/.

14 Report from a Story in TV GuideNews on July 28, 2015. https://www.tvguide.com/news/donald-trump-presidential-campaign-timeline/.

15 Ibid, (p. 9).

16 Ibid, (p. 8).

17 Appelbaum, Y. (2016, July 21). I alone can fix it. *The Atlantic*. www.theatlantic.com/politics/archive/2016/07/trump-rnc-speech-alone-fix-it/492557/.

18 Trump, D. J. (2015, June 16). Here's Donald Trump's presidential announcement speech. *Time website* (Speech audio recording). https://time.com/3923128/donald-trump-announcement-speech/.

19 Reported by NBC News on See https://www.nbcnews.com/politics/donald-trump/trump-suggests-injection-disinfectant-beat-coronavirus-clean-lungs-n1191216.

20 Retrieved from https://thehill.com/homenews/administration/437610-trump-calls-press-the-enemy-of-the-people/.

21 Ibid.

22 The source for the statistics is the Pew Research Center. https://www.pewresearch.org/politics/2023/09/19/public-trust-in-government-1958-2023/.

23 Ibid.

24 Fahrenthold, D. A. (2016, October 8). Trump recorded having extremely lewd conversation about women in 2005. *Washington Post*. In October 2016, a clip from a Trump interview with Access Hollywood host Billy Bush revealed Trump "bragged in vulgar terms about kissing, groping, and trying to have sex with women during a 2005 conversation caught on a hot microphone, saying that 'when you're a star, they let you do it,' according to a video obtained by The Washington Post." https://www.washingtonpost.com/politics/trump-recorded-having-extremely-lewd-conversation-about-women-in-2005/2016/10/07/3b9ce776-8cb4-11e6-bf8a-3d26847eeed4_story.html.

25 Beckett, L. (2017, March 30). Evangelical Christian leaders: Travel ban violates religious belief of refugees. *The Guardian*. https://www.theguardian.com/us-news/2017/jan/30/evangelical-christians-trump-travel-ban-christian-refugees.

26 McCammon, S. (2016, June 21). Inside Trump's closed-door meeting, held to reassure 'the Evangelicals'. *NPR*. https://www.theguardian.com/us-news/2017/jan/30/evangelical-christians-trump-travel-ban-christian-refugees.

27 The American roots of this experience dating back to the 1920s can be found at *Dionne, E. J. "Culture Wars: How 2004"*.

Reference List

Appelbaum, Y. (2016, July 21). I alone can fix it. *The Atlantic*.

Beckett, L. (2017, March 30). Evangelical Christian leaders: Travel ban violates religious belief of refugees. *The Guardian*. https://www.theguardian.com/us-news/2017/jan/30/evangelical-christians-trump-travel-ban-christian-refugees.

Fahrenthold, D. A. (October 8, 2016). Trump recorded having extremely lewd conversation about women in 2005. *Washington Post*. https://www.washingtonpost.com/politics/trump-recorded-having-extremely-lewd-conversation-about-women-in-2005/2016/10/07/3b9ce776-8cb4-11e6-bf8a-3d26847eeed4_story.html.

Haberman, M. (2022). *Confidence man*. New York, NY: Penguin Press.

MacGregor, J. R. (2019). *Trump the biography*. Sheridan, WY: CAC Publishing LLC.

McCammon, S. (2016, June 21). Inside Trump's closed-door meeting, held to reassure 'the Evangelicals'. *NPR*. https://www.theguardian.com/us-news/2017/jan/30/evangelical-christians-trump-travel-ban-christian-refugees.

Trump, D. J. (2015, June 16). Here's Donald Trump's presidential announcement speech. *Time website* (Speech audio recording). https://time.com/3923128/donald-trump-announcement-speech/.

Trump, D. J., and Schwartz, T. (1987). *The art of the deal*. New York, NY: Ballantine Books.

4 Charismatic bonds and religious followers

How charismatic leaders build relationships with religious followers

Breaking from the status quo is a prime characteristic of a charismatic leader. As a radical change agent, this kind of leader is uniquely equipped to muster the energy in his followers "to break with the established order, provide for its members' basic everyday needs, fend off outside threats, and institutionalize a new utopia."[1] In this manner, charisma springs from an affinity, or closeness, that creates a bond stemming from a "highly charged, interlocking relationship of positive effect."[2] We distinguish communities from communion in that the former are structures to foster a sense of belonging, whereas communion is the act of creating a deep connection among participants. This more profound level, called "communion, releases the energy locked up in established social patterns."[3] It is highly volatile. However, it is stabilized by the powerful bond that members call grace. So, charisma is an "emergent system, with properties independent of the characteristics of individuals,"[4] which raises followers to extraordinary levels of commitment.

The essence of church congregations is centered on spending time together, called fellowship, an essential function of religious communities. Communion extends to a deeper level. It is not hierarchical but a "relatively undifferentiated . . . communion of equal individuals."[5] In communion—being in union—the group "acts as a powerful reflector in which each round of interaction is self-reinforcing, building quickly by a process of emotional contagion to higher levels of intensity."[6] It releases energy previously locked up in social conventions and "is like a reaction chamber of free-flowing, spontaneous reaction,"[7] a powerful relationship of leadership that is prone to occur between charismatics and their followers, so strong that "followers place their destiny in his hands. It is as if they have fallen under a magical spell; they become submissive, obedient, enraptured—blind in their absolute loyalty. His authority over them seems boundless."[8]

The charismatic relationship between leader and follower results from the follower aligning with the leader in two ways, either voluntarily or through

DOI: 10.4324/9781003463047-5

unquestioning acceptance. The nature of the follower drives these options and determines when they choose to follow. Consider the two types of charismatic leadership at the center of this work: personalized and socialized. Personalized leaders "articulate goals that are leader-driven and recognize followers' needs only to the degree necessary to achieve their goals. They objectify their followers, viewing them as objects to be manipulated."[9] Examples include Hitler, Polpot, and Jim Jones.

Socialized leaders "articulate follower-driven goals, recognize followers' needs, and help them develop in their own right." Examples include Ronald Reagan, Winston Churchill, and John F. Kennedy. These two types are qualitatively different in their use of power, to benefit either themselves (personalized) or their followers (socialized).[10] Additionally, whether it is voluntarily or through unquestioning acceptance is predicated on the personality traits of followers, such as (a) high or low self-esteem, self-confidence, independence, or dependence;[11] (b) self-concept clarity and self-monitoring;[12] and (c) expressive or instrumental orientation, pragmatic or principled, and values and identity.[13] For our purposes, we will focus on high-esteem and low-esteem followers.

Determining what types of people become followers of charismatics and when is a question best framed in four different situations related to the existence of a crisis and the level of esteem in the follower: (a) crisis and low self-esteem followers; (b) crisis and high self-esteem followers; (c) non-crisis or opportunistic situation and low self-esteem followers; and (d) non-crisis or opportunistic situation and high self-esteem followers. In short, low self-esteem followers in crisis offer obedience because they seek help dealing with the threat represented in the situation.

In contrast, high self-esteem followers in a crisis do not focus on negative thoughts after failure but on their strengths, making them less likely to be persuaded by imminent threats. Hence, under crises, low-esteem followers are more likely to accept or obey personalized charismatics, and high-esteem followers are not. Further, in crisis, the socialized leader is more likely to focus primarily on the crisis, so high-esteem followers are less likely to be influenced by them.

In non-crisis (opportunistic) situations, high-esteem followers are more likely to voluntarily accept socialized charismatics because the leader links followers' values and purpose with a compelling vision. They tend to reject those leaders focused on power to benefit themselves, knowing they can be successful without submitting to a leader. Low self-esteem followers under non-crisis or opportunistic situations will not be as vulnerable to with type as they do not perceive the threat. This framework is noteworthy because it illuminates how charismatic leaders build potent relationships with religious followers. Understanding how followers engage charismatic leaders sheds light on how and why charismatic leaders can generate uncommonly high commitment from followers. As explained here, followers are moved by the communion that is ignited by the leader's charisma, and we now know that personalized leaders tend to draw from low-esteem followers seeking shelter from the storm. High-esteem followers are likelier to engage socialized leaders but not with the same intensity.

The role of religious rhetoric and symbolism in fostering loyalty

Religions worldwide face various challenges characterized by crises, reflecting broad and diverse issues concerning their role in society, their influence on followers' decisions, and the relationship between church and state. These challenges vary significantly between different religious groups and regions and influence the role and perception of religion in contemporary society.

While some skepticism exists about the co-mingled relationship between church and state, they exist in a nested reality. That is, it is sometimes difficult to recognize the boundaries of each because one feeds upon the other. Religion extends its influence beyond providing a collective identity by embedding a moral and ethical framework within the nation.

Religious principles frequently permeate legal systems and social policies, fostering a sense of moral purpose that becomes synonymous with nationalistic ideals. Religious phrases and symbols are incorporated into governmental artifacts, like the phrase *In God We Trust* that is inscribed on all US currency; the phrase "under God" was added to the Pledge of Allegiance in 1954, during the Cold War; and it is incorporated into the design of federal buildings, including the Supreme Court which features the Ten Commandments in a frieze inside the courtroom.

Christian values have historically shaped the political discourse and social policies, reinforcing a national narrative aligning with religious doctrines and legitimizing political power in the United States. Political leaders and movements often harness religious symbolism and rhetoric to justify their authority, claiming divine sanction for their governance. This strategy reinforces their political power and strengthens nationalistic sentiments, making the populace more cohesive and aligned with the government's agenda.

However, the relationship between religion and nationalism is not without its complexities, especially when a candidate appropriates nationalism as a preferred way of life, as Trump did in 2015 at the outset of his campaign. While religion can unify, it can also alienate. It often defines national identity in a way that marginalizes or alienates those who do not conform to the dominant religious norms, creating stark divisions within societies and dissonance among members of organized religions.

This dynamic of nationalism is evident in Israel, where Jewish religious identity is deeply entwined with nationalistic policies and societal norms, affecting everything from citizenship to public life. When there is a nearly synonymous nature between church and state, it introduces complexity and potentially mixed signals, with the potential to favor in-group believers against out-group non-believers. In Israel's case, Christians in the United States formally support Israel as they see the Holy Land in Israel and a shared foundation of Hebrew Scriptures and The Old Testament. Yet, from a doctrinal point of view, they differ significantly. Jews see Jesus Christ as a Holy Man, akin to a rabbi, whereas Christians see Jesus Christ as divine, the son of God. Suffice it to say, symbols and icons generate shared feelings and emotions with which followers of different religions may see similarly, offering skilled rhetoricians rich opportunities to fashion a language of shared values that appeal universally.

While religion can unify a nation around shared beliefs and customs, it can also lead to the exclusion or marginalization of those who do not share the dominant religious identity. This can reinforce a sense of "us" versus "them" when national identity becomes inextricably linked to religious identity. In other places worldwide, political leaders have mobilized followers into a political religion imposed by the state. "Hitlerism, Nazism, communism. They were political religions. They were much more violent, and that is precisely the transformation that happened to Putinism."[14] Political religions began as civil religions "with quasi-religious rituals, ideas that were optional for Russian people. Now, it's not optional anymore."[15] This is an example of a fusion of church and state, where the political leader uses religion to extend his coercive power.

This narrative comes from a book written by Tim Alberta, author of *The Kingdom, The Power, and the Glory*, a book that ties right-wing extremism to the current estate of evangelicalism, that suggests the Church has been "captured by nationalist ideals . . . [and that] Christian nationalism was now 'the predominant form of evangelical Christianity' in the United States."[16] He cites Cyril Hovorun, a Russian Orthodox monk who has experienced such phenomena firsthand in Russia, where a political religion emerged to advance secular interests. At a global conference, Hovorun was asked if, given that Putinism was a secular religion he saw in Russia, he saw the same forces at play with Trumpism in the United States. The monk replied that political beliefs are imposed and tend to be violent, which is not the case in the United States. Yet he believed that Christianity was becoming less Christ-centered; he said,

> I've come to believe . . . that the Christ of the gospel has become a moral stranger to us. . . . If you read the gospels, the things that profoundly mattered to Christ, they marginally mattered to most evangelical Christians.[17]

Alberta sounds an alarm about one aspect of this increasingly blurred relationship:

> Religion and politics are natural enemies; both give the masses a sense of belonging and self-actualization. Tension between the two is healthy and necessary. When one appropriates the other, history shows that oppression—leading to death and human suffering at a woeful scale—is the inevitable result.[18]

He cites the work of Miroslav Volf, a theologian who heads Yale University's Center for Faith and Culture. The son of a Pentecostal minister in Croatia, Volf grew up in a region comprised of Bosnia and Herzegovina (Muslim), Serbia (Orthodox), and Croatia (Catholic), where all "preached dogmatic nationalism as Yugoslavia careened toward civil war in the late 1980s."[19] Volf witnessed "creeping totalitarianism in the name of religious conviction."[20] This manifests when leaders (a) place cultural identity over a shared community, (b) stress the purification of those identities, and (c) when violence becomes legitimized for the protection of group identities. The message here is that religion can, and has, been subsumed by politics when the church is "captured by nationalist ideals."[21]

Comparative analysis of Obama and Trump strategies in engaging religious communities

We live in an over-communicated society, and the challenge is not reading all the messages; it is deciding which are worthy to note and accurately deciphering their meaning. Leaders play a significant role in narrowing the choices for people. When a leader articulates an idea that strikes a chord with a follower, they are moved to believe and act in accordance with the leader's vision. When this connection moves a follower to identify with the leader and emulate them, a psychological concept called transference has likely occurred. It involves redirecting feelings and desires, particularly those unconsciously retained from childhood, toward a new object, such as a psychotherapist, during therapy sessions. However, it is not limited to therapy and can occur in interpersonal relationships. Charismatic leaders often inspire strong feelings and deep admiration from their followers, creating an ideal scenario for transference.

Barack Obama

As a community organizer in Chicago, Obama went into primarily African American enclaves to organize the Developing Communities Project, a church-funded effort. He experienced the contrast between his upbringing, devoid of organized religion, and the engagement he witnessed in religious congregations, such as the one he claimed as his, the Trinity United Church of Christ. Obama's relationship with his church was rooted more in personal convictions than congregational relationships.

Charismatic leaders adeptly cultivate relationships with religious followers by deploying a multifaceted approach that resonates on spiritual, emotional, and communal levels. These relationships' core is the alignment of shared values and beliefs. Charismatic leaders effectively articulate values that mirror what their religious followers hold, reinforcing trust and establishing a deep connection based on shared moral and ethical ground. These leaders are also visionary, often framing their objectives for a higher purpose that frequently aligns with religious teachings or the associated moral imperatives. His relationships with two prominent religious leaders explain Obama's stance on religion and religious followers' connection to Obama.

Obama's core theme of hope was a means to connect with similar messages expounded by Roman Catholic Pope Francis. Each man articulated a vision of a better future and emphasized the role of individual responsibility in achieving broader societal or global goals. Both leaders used hope to inspire and motivate, but they did so in different arenas—one religious and the other secular. Therefore, their approaches converge in their belief that hope is essential to facing and overcoming adversity. Obama and Pope Francis both articulate a vision of a better future and emphasize the role of individual responsibility in achieving broader societal or global goals.

Pope Francis and Barack Obama also met several times, discussing various global issues such as poverty, climate change, and immigration—areas where they both seek to inspire hope for positive change.

Figure 4.1 shows the pair of leaders in one of their face-to-face encounters that highlighted mutual respect and shared commitment to values that foster hope and action toward a more just and sustainable world captured in this

Figure 4.1 Obama connecting with religious icon

statement: "The fact is, the challenges we face today from saving our planet to ending poverty are simply too big for government to solve alone. . . . We need all hands on deck."[22] Thus, while their contexts might differ, their connection through the theme of hope was evident in their leadership and public discourse, resonating across different audiences worldwide.

Billy Graham was a religious leader whose primary concern was spreading the Christian gospel. He was known for his apolitical stance in his revivals, though he was conservative in his political views. Graham was an icon for inspiring presidential providence. He counseled presidents from both parties, maintaining a more spiritual than politically partisan role. His focus was on personal transformation through faith rather than specific policy advocacy. So, despite their differences, Obama and Graham were united in this mission. They shared some common values, particularly regarding ethical leadership and the importance of faith in public life. Both emphasized the moral dimensions of leadership and the role of personal integrity and humility.

The emotional bonds between charismatic leaders and their religious followers are further strengthened through powerful oratory and personal charisma. These leaders forge a profound emotional resonance by using narratives rich with spiritual symbolism and metaphors that speak to the followers' spiritual experiences. This connection is not superficial but woven into the fabric of the followers' spiritual and emotional lives. In this, Obama appeared authentic in his religious beliefs. This departs from the idea that professional speechwriters largely control what a candidate says and dispels the notion that the skill of speechwriters supersedes the core values and charisma of the leader. Like a Sunday preacher, Obama prepared his "sermons" and was rewarded with the authentic label. The Obama campaign "raised eyebrows and elicited snickers when unveiled the Obamamania version of the presidential seal."[23] Appropriating official government symbols was a bridge too far, and the Obama team withdrew it as fast as it was unveiled.

Donald J. Trump

Though not distinguished as policy-driven by Washington Beltway standards, Trump's presidency resonated with Christians, particularly Evangelicals. Trump's distinctive speaking style—simple, blunt, and short on details but high on hyperbole and repetition—resulted in pleasing platitudes that addressed Christian values and concerns, that is, anti-abortion, which he characteristically reshaped over time. In 1999, he stated: "I hate abortion. I hate it. I hate everything it stands for. I cringe when I listen to people debating the subject. But you still—I just believe in choice." [24] By 2016, he called for punishment of any woman who had an abortion. This move to a more strident and jarring position characteristically evoked the PCL style of eschewing obfuscation. This expression foreshadowed to Christians that he was a no-nonsense leader, later reinforced by appointing conservative judges to the Supreme Court and other federal courts, creating a potential pathway to overturn Roe v. Wade.

Christian followers welcomed the appointments of conservative judges Neil Gorsuch, Brett Kavanaugh, and Amy Coney Barrett as critical steps toward restoring fundamental values. These appointments to the US Supreme Court shifted its balance to the right, leading to the Dobbs decision, overturning Roe v. Wade removing the federal guarantee to a woman's right to an abortion by shifting the authority to individual states.

Regarding foreign policy decisions, Christians hailed his unwavering support for Israel. Further, in true charismatic-leader fashion, he magnified his support by announcing he would move the US Embassy to Jerusalem, a decision Evangelical Christians viewed as fulfilling biblical prophecy essential to their theological perspective.

He directed his administration to protect individuals and businesses that refused services based on religious beliefs, which he framed as a battle against a tide of secularism. Trump's vice president, Mike Pence, was a touchstone of credibility that tightened the bond with evangelical Christians. Pence vigorously reinforced Trump's commitment at religious gatherings and evangelical conferences. In an under-the-radar manner, Pence defined the role of a Trump surrogate, in this case, giving testimony to Trump's direct commitment to Christians.

Pence's involvement was a touchstone of Christian victories during Trump's tenure. There is little doubt that Pence served as a moral counterweight for evangelical Christians who harbored reservations about Trump's personal history and demeanor and gave rise to the notion he was a God-sent change agent. Pence, perceived as holy and devout, provided a reassuring balance to Trump's more controversial persona. For Evangelicals who sought a leader who embodied their religious and moral values, Pence was a beacon drawing attention to the underlying force of change, Donald J. Trump. Make no mistake, Pence was the drawing card for the main show.

Trump's bond with Christians held firm even after Trump distanced himself from Pence after he refused to reject the Electoral College vote affirming Biden's win. By then, Trump had successfully positioned himself as a staunch advocate of Christian beliefs.

Trump's rhetoric and public declarations often included themes of Christian nationalism, portraying him as a defender of Christian values against liberal elites perceived as hostile to traditional Christian ways of life in America. This narrative found resonance with Christians who felt culturally and socially marginalized in an increasingly secular society. Significant endorsements from prominent Christian leaders and evangelical figureheads also played a critical role. Figure 4.2 is a photo opportunity that Trump effectively used to substantiate his commitment to Christians.

Many charismatic leaders used their influence within their communities and networks to legitimize Trump's candidacy and presidency, amplifying his policies and views as a reflection of Christian doctrine. Trump leveraged this

Impression management executed through photo opportunity of symbolic unity

President Trump prays with African American leaders on February 27, 2020 Photo Credit: Chip Somodevilla

Figure 4.2 Trump connecting in Oval Office with religious followers

alignment to his advantage, not by professing to live the values but by being a staunch defender of followers who held those values. This proved to be a highly effective way for Trump to create a communal bond energized by Trump's charismatic appeal. This took on a life of its own through endorsements by others and by incorporating church rituals and symbols into his campaign.

Trump's rallies have always been a defining characteristic of his impression management strategy. Ever the entertainer, Trump created a very effective traveling showcase, the Trump Rally. Trump saw the value of cozying up to the "faithful" back in 2021 when he deftly positioned himself as a humble protector: "This country has a savior, and it's not me—that's someone much higher up than me," he extolled from the pulpit at First Baptist Church in Dallas, whose congregation exceeds 14,000 people.[24] Drawing on third-party validation in 2023, Representative Marjorie Taylor Greene, a Georgia Republican and a close Trump ally, said both the former president and Jesus had been arrested by "radical, corrupt governments." Playing on the persecution theme, Trump shared an article on social media with the headline "The Crucifixion of Donald Trump."[25] In 2024, *The New York Times* wrote a story called *The Church of Trump*, illustrating how he appropriated elements of Christian rituals into his rallies, like the somber music and alter call to close out his rally. Then, in 2024, he offered himself willingly, "In the end, they are not after me. They are after you. I just happen to be standing in their way, and I always will."[26] Finally, days before Easter 2024, he introduced the Trump Bible, which included copies of some of the nation's founding documents and handwritten lyrics to Lee Greenwood's song "God Bless the U.S.A."[27]

Many are confused that devout Christians can so readily perceive him as a savior and are confused about how he can gloss over his propensity to stretch the truth, womanize, and ruthlessly challenge the law. However, his Christian followers are more likely to describe him as a modern version of Old Testament heroes like Cyrus or David, morally flawed figures handpicked by God to lead profound missions to achieve overdue justice or resist existential evil. "He's been chosen by God," said Marie Zere, a commercial real estate broker from Long Island who attended the Conservative Political Action Conference in February outside Washington, DC. "He's still surviving even though all these people are coming after him, and I don't know how else to explain that other than divine intervention."

Cementing his charismatic credentials as one willing to make personal sacrifices on behalf of his followers, he holds up the political attacks and legal peril he faces, which are nothing short of biblical. "They've crucified him worse than Jesus,"[28] said Andriana Howard, 67, who works as a restaurant food runner in Conway, SC. This metaphor of persecution serves to connect Trump to the role that a truth-teller often suffers when their message threatens others, which serves to more deeply embed Trump's assertion that he is the truth that corrupt people loathe.

Trump's braiding of politics and religion is hardly a new phenomenon. Christianity has long strongly influenced the American government, with most voters identifying as Christians even as the country grows more secular. According to Gallup, 68% of adults said they were Christian in 2022, down from 91% in 1948. This may be another reason Evangelicals have sidled up with the former president, who has methodically established himself as the one true Republican leader whose religious overtones have pervaded his third presidential campaign.

Benevolently phrased fundraising emails in his name promise unconditional love amid solicitations for contributions of as little as $5.

Russell Moore, the former president of the Southern Baptist Convention's public-policy arm, said Mr. Trump's rallies had veered into "dangerous territory" with the altar call closing and opening prayers from preachers describing Mr. Trump as heaven-sent. "Claiming godlike authority or an endorsement from God for a political candidate means that person cannot be questioned or opposed without also opposing God," Mr. Moore said. "That's a violation of the commandment to not take the Lord's name in vain."

In summary, developing a collective identity is crucial in the dynamics between charismatic leaders and their followers. Through shared experiences and consistent interaction, leaders foster a sense of unity centered around common religious and spiritual values, enhancing group cohesion and loyalty. Sometimes, leaders extend their influence by providing spiritual guidance and deepening their relationships as followers view them as leaders and spiritual mentors. This role transformation is significant, marking the leader's influence as profoundly impactful on both the personal and communal levels.

Charismatic leaders construct robust and enduring relationships with their religious followers through these strategies, characterized by shared values, emotional connections, and a collective sense of purpose. These relationships are not merely transactional but are profoundly transformative, influencing both the leaders and the followers in profound ways and often driving significant social and political movements.

It is this alignment of the leader's personal skills and inherent understanding of the wiring of followers' needs. It wants to yield the kind of outsized allegiance found in charismatic leadership arrangements, particularly concerning religious groups so tied to their beliefs. The value of comparing these two leaders provides deep insight into how high-functioning leadership works and, more importantly, a clear understanding of the communication tools and tactics each leader employs to coalesce a shared sense of meaning, direction, and commitment in accomplishing desired outcomes.

Notes

1 Bradley, T. B. (1999). *Charisma and social structure*. New York, NY: toExcel, p. 79.
2 Ibid, (p. 80).
3 Ibid.
4 Ibid, (p. 9).
5 Turner, V. W. (1969). *The ritual process: Structure and anti-structure*. Chicago, IL: Aldine Publishing Co, pp. 126–127.
6 Bradley (1999), (p. 107).
7 Ibid, (p. 108).
8 Ibid, (p. 49).
9 Kyoungsu, K., Dansereau, F., and Kom, I. (2002). Charismatic leadership: Three dimensions of charismatic leadership. In B. J. Avolio, and F. J. Yammarino (Eds.), *Transformational and charismatic leadership: The road ahead*. JAI, an Imprint of Elsevier, pp. 146–172.
10 McClelland, D. C. (1975). *Power: The inner experience*. New York, NY: Irvington.
11 Conger, J. A. (1989). *The charismatic leader: Behind the mystique of exceptional leadership*. San Francisco, CA: Jossey-Bass.
12 Weierter, S. J. M. (1997). Who wants to play follow the leader? A theory of charismatic relationships based on routinized charisma and follower characteristics. *Leadership Quarterly,* 8, 171–193.
13 Klein, K. J., and House, R. J. (1995). On fire: Charismatic leadership and levels of analysis. *The Leadership Quarterly,* 6, 163–198.
14 Alberta, T. (2023). *The kingdom, the power, and the glory*. New York, NY: HarperCollins, p. 241.
15 Ibid, (p. 240).
16 Ibid.
17 Ibid, (p. 241).

18 Alberta (2023), (pp. 237–238).
19 Ibid, (p. 235).
20 Ibid, (p. 236).
21 Ibid, (p. 240).
22 Zeleny, J., and Knowlton, B. (2008, July 2). Obama wants to expand role of religious groups. *The New York Times*. https://www.nytimes.com/2008/07/02/us/politics/02campaigncnd.html.
23 Smith-Schoenwalder, S. April 8, 2024. QUOTES: Comparing Trump's stance on abortion over time. U.S. News & World Report. https://www.usnews.com/news/national-news/articles/quotes-comparing-trumps-stance-on-abortion-over-time.
24 New York Daily News (01/12, 2019). Barack Obama appears with personalized presidential seal.
25 Ibid.
26 Bender, M. C. (2024, April 1). The church of Trump: How he's infusing Christianity into his movement. *New York Times*. https://www.nytimes.com/2024/04/01/us/politics/trump-2024-religion.html?searchResultPosition=2.
27 Ibid.
28 Ibid.

Reference List

Alberta, T. (2023). *The kingdom, the power, and the glory*. New York, NY: HarperCollins.

Bender, M. C. (2024, April 1). The church of Trump: How he's infusing Christianity into his movement. *New York Times*. https://www.nytimes.com/2024/04/01/us/politics/trump-2024-religion.html?searchResultPosition=2.

Bradley, T. B. (1987/1999). *Charisma and social structure: A study of love and power, wholeness and transformation*. New York, NY: toExcel.

Klein, K. J., and House, R. J. (1995). On fire: Charismatic leadership and levels of analysis. *The Leadership Quarterly,* 6, 163–198.

Kyoungsu, K., Dansereau, F., and Kim, I. (2002). Charismatic leadership: Three dimensions of charismatic leadership. In B. J. Avolio, and F. J. Yammarino (Eds.), *Transformational and charismatic leadership: The road ahead*. Oxford, UK: JAI, an Imprint of Elsevier, pp. 146–172.

McClelland, D. C. (1975). *Power: The inner experience*. New York, NY: Irvington.

Raven, B. H. (1992). The bases of power: Origins and recent developments. *Journal of Social Issues*, 49(4). pp. 227–251. https://doi.org/10.1111/j.1540-4560.1993.tb01191.x.

Smith-Schoenwalder, S. (2024, April 8). QUOTES: Comparing Trump's stance on abortion over time. *U.S. News & World Report*. https://www.usnews.com/news/national-news/articles/quotes-comparing-trumps-stance-on-abortion-over-time.

Turner, V. W. (1969). *The ritual process: Structure and anti-structure*. Chicago, IL: Aldine Publishing Co.

Weierter, S. J. M. (1997). Who wants to play follow the leader? A throaty of charismatic relationships based on routinized charisma and follower characteristics. *Leadership Quarterly,* 8, 171–193.

Zeleny, J., and Knowlton, B. (2008, July 2). Obama wants to expand the role of religious groups. *The New York Times*. https://www.nytimes.com/2008/07/02/us/politics/02campaigncnd.html.

5 The power of charisma in political mobilization

Understanding how politicians mobilize their base

Politics is how societies and groups make decisions and involve various activities, from debating laws, negotiating with other political entities, and campaigning for positions. The late Speaker of the House Tip O'Neill, famously said, "All politics is local." He meant that a politician's success is directly tied to their ability to understand and influence their constituents on issues that matter to them. Success pivots on the premise that a person seeking office must understand the everyday concerns of the people they represent, such as their safety, economic well-being, personal freedoms, and overall quality of life. So, local means national and international politics.

To understand how this political interplay can impact the local way of life, consider the city-wide anti-fracking referendum passed in Denton, Texas, in 2014. Texas Governor Greg Abbott and the Texas legislature superseded the ordinance by passing a state law that forbade local entities from banning fracking. When questioned if it was hypocritical for the state to limit city power over local issues, Abbott flipped the issue:

> We have sued the federal government multiple times because of the heavy hand of regulation from the federal government—trying to run individuals' lives, infringing upon individual liberty. . . . At the same time, we are ensuring that people and officials at the local level are not going to be infringing upon individual liberty or individual rights.[1]

Abbott's pivoting of a local control argument to that of protecting liberties is an example of skilled manipulation of public opinion that re-positions issues to reverse local decisions. It is a political skill that Abbott employs to this day.

Politicians manage public opinion primarily through communication strategies, including messaging, media appearances, public speeches, and social media engagement. They craft narratives that resonate with voters' values and concerns, use targeted advertising to reach specific audiences, and respond to public issues that align with or shape public sentiment. Additionally, politicians

DOI: 10.4324/9781003463047-6

often engage with key influencers and opinion leaders to amplify their messages and manage public perception to support their stance, which is powerful. Public Relations pioneer Edward Bernays wrote:

> The conscious and intelligent manipulation of the organized habits and opinions of the masses is an essential element in a democratic society. Those who manipulate this unseen mechanism of society constitute an invisible government, which is the true ruling power of our country.[2]

Bernays discovered the power of this kind of mass persuasion when he engineered the *Torches of Freedom in 1929.* The American Tobacco Company hired Bernays to encourage women's smoking by exploiting their right to a better life when it was considered a social taboo for women to smoke cigarettes. He hired women to march in the New York Easter Day Parade, smoking cigarettes every step of the way as a means to publicly demonstrate smoking as a personal freedom. The stunt begged the question, why not let women smoke? It is their right. It was considered the first wave of feminism in the United States.

The scheme sprang from a clever notion proffered by Walter Lippman, a writer, reporter, and political commentator, that "people's view of reality was guided by the 'pictures in their heads.'"[3] These pseudo-environments, he believed, could help people see their "larger political environment . . . more successfully."[4] Lippman, a socialist, re-imagined the word "stereotype" to mean "a repertory of fixed impressions . . . we carry around in our heads."[5]

He believed stereotypes existed in the culture and were drawn upon by the human mind to help articulate the meaning of the human experience. He argued, "Stereotypes constituted a coherent—if inaccurate—worldview. Unconsciously, but aggressively, people relied on them to sense where they belong."[6] In short, stereotypes govern perception. They leverage commonly held beliefs or perceptions to convey a message quickly and effectively. Lippman warned, "There is one danger in using stereotypes by the public relations counsel. That . . . demagogues in every field of social relationship can take advantage of the public."[7]

Trump made regular use of stereotypes to polarize and mobilize his followers. For example, during the COVID-19 pandemic, Trump repeatedly referred to the coronavirus as the "China virus" or "Kung Flu," which critics argued used racial stereotypes to blame the pandemic on Chinese people and divert attention from his administration's handling of the crisis. In 2015, Trump used stereotypes to support his proposal for a "total and complete shutdown of Muslims entering the United States." This proposal played into fears and stereotypes about Muslims as potential terrorists, contributing to significant controversy and criticism.[8] He often described African American communities in stereotypical terms as rife with poverty, crime, and despair. He would then ask for their vote, "What do you have to lose?"[9]

As Lippman advised, stereotypes are coherent but not necessarily accurate. Nonetheless, they are potent tools to galvanize public opinion. When used ethically, it can positively affect society, but the contrary is also true.

Obama's rhetoric avoided stereotypes, focusing on inclusivity, unity, and respect for diversity. He often used precise language to address complex issues, acknowledging the nuances in policy discussions or debates. For example, when discussing terrorism, he was careful to distinguish between the actions of extremist groups and the beliefs of the broader Muslim community. At a CNN Town Hall meeting in 2016, he clarified his stance:

> There is no doubt, and I've said repeatedly, where we see terrorist organizations like al Qaeda or ISIL. They have perverted and distorted and tried to claim the mantle of Islam for an excuse for basically barbarism and death. . . . These are people who've killed children, killed Muslims, take sex slaves, there's no religious rationale that would justify in any way any of the things that they do, ... But what I have been careful about when I describe these issues is to make sure that we do not lump these murderers into the billion Muslims that exist around the world, including in this country, who are peaceful, who are responsible, who, in this country, are fellow troops and police officers and firefighters and teachers and neighbors and friends.[10]

Stereotypes effectively mobilize people into action by simplifying complex issues and activating strong emotional responses. Avoiding their use removes a tool of shorthand that is an effective conduit of meaning.

Politicians face problems. Voters measure their elected officials on their ability to deal with problems. Often, the problem is technical, as is experienced when the mayor sees that the trash is picked up on time and streets are made to channel traffic efficiently. Technical problems rely on existing knowledge and authoritative expertise for resolution. The second is the adaptive challenge, which demands changes in people's mindsets, behaviors, and social practices, requiring collaborative exploration and new learning. That demands leadership skills.

All leaders exercise power. In their seminal work, French and Raven (1959) and a follow-up study by Raven (1993) identified six bases of power that served as a model for studying power and how it is connected to leadership. They are (a) expert, based on perceived competence; (b) referent, based on liking the leader; (c) reward, based on what the leader may offer; (d) coercive, based on the penalties a leader may deal out; (e) legitimate, based on the internalization of shared values;[11] and (f) informational (persuasion).[12] A leader benefits when they can recognize the power available to them and can combine one or more of these elements into a disciplined approach to exercising authority.

"Long linked to the exercise of authority or influence, . . .[leadership] usually suggests playing a prominent and coordinating role in an organization or society . . . [captured] in the word 'mobilize.'"[13] In this context, "leadership is an activity—the activity of a citizen from any walk of life mobilizing people to do something."[14] Imagine, then, that a leader's effectiveness is multiplied when they recognize their goals must reflect the needs of both the leader and the follower. "The two essentials of power are motive and resource. The two are interrelated. Lacking motive, resource diminishes; lacking resource, motive lies idle."[15]

With the sources of power in mind, we can examine how leaders marshal their authority to realize their vision and accomplish their goals. Power is the potential influence that one has, and generally, "the one with the power has control over something the other person (or group) desires. The common theme . . . is that objectives were attained (or behavior was changed) because of an influencing party."[16] The source of power "may lie in the immense reserves of the wants and needs of the wielders and objects of power, just as the winds and tides, oil and coal, the atom and the sun have been harnessed to supply physical energy."[17]

In politics, the influencing party employs informal or referent power, which may be derived from a mix of the aforementioned elements. It is not dependent on the leader holding a formal title so much as commanding the leadership skills discussed. So, to think politically, one must understand the stakeholders involved. That means knowing their needs and desired outcomes, their level of engagement, and the degree of power and authority they may grant the leader to solve their problems. This process hinges on learning what each constituent group values, to whom they are loyal, and the degree of their passion for what they care about. Consider this:

> The key assumption behind thinking politically is that people in an organization seek to meet the expectations of their constituencies. When you understand the nature of these expectations, you can mobilize people effectively.[18]

There are two kinds of challenges: technical and adaptive. Technical challenges "can be diagnosed and solved, generally within a short time frame, by applying established know-how and procedures."[19] Adaptive challenges are more complex as no proven routinized means to assure a solution exists. The problem is a gap between what people believe is thriving and the reality they face, requiring political skills and the ability to interpret the situation effectively. Moreover, it is often the case that "closing the gap between the espoused and the current reality . . . would be more painful to the dominant coalition than living with it."[20]

The most common cause of failure in leadership is when leaders attempt to treat adaptive problems with technical applications. Hence,

> Adaptive challenges can only be addressed through changes in people's priorities, beliefs, habits, and loyalties. Making progress goes beyond any

> authoritative expertise to mobilize discovery, shedding certain entrenched ways, tolerating losses, and generating new capacity to thrive anew.[21]

Candidates are elected to public office by "telling constituents that they will not have to suffer losses to meet the challenges at hand."[22] After the 9/11 attacks, Americans wanted stability again without paying a price that would disrupt their sense of thriving. Politicians on both sides of the fence "colluded to perpetuate that fantasy. . . . The preferred message was, 'Resume your lives. The government will go after the perpetrators and take care of the problem.'" Sure, there will be losses exhibited by the courageous who will fight on the front lines, but casualties will be kept at a minimum, and we will return to our lives as before the attack.

Americans welcomed these messages but, at the very least, were severely unrealistic. As it turns out, recovery from the 9/11 attacks was not a technical challenge; it required an adaptive response, one that would demand leadership that would draw upon the best from the country's traditions, identity, and history to fashion a future state of thriving. It was not the kind of challenge that leaders relish. This required a compelling vision.

Charismatic leaders are better equipped to deal with adaptive challenges as they are gifted at envisioning and mustering the confidence of followers once they have identified and communicated a discrepant view of the challenge that resonated with followers. The second part is more challenging. Adaptation requires learning new ways, identifying those attachments that no longer serve the purpose, and shifting the mindset from conflict avoidance to conflict resolution.[23] Adaptive problems rely on the leader reframing interpretations, the patterns of behavior that help make sense of a situation. This is accomplished by "explaining raw data through digestible understandings and narratives."[24]

Successful politicians begin with a vision that rings true with followers and is presented with sufficient imagination to generate appeal. Providing an interpretation of a problem or challenge is a means to deal with competing interests and contrasting expectations of various groups. In other words, there will be winners and losers on every issue, and losers are quick to turn on the leader who fails to deliver on their expectations. The challenge for the leader is to frame their decisions to allow them to take the high ground and be perceived as honest with followers' best interests at heart.

By identifying the values most closely held by followers—the thing they care about the most—the leader must be able to navigate a path that presents a higher-level value that was served even though a lower-level value was sacrificed. Think of taking a position on a controversial topic like abortion/choice. When forced, Trump was best served by presenting the issue not as a pro-life/pro-choice binary decision but instead as of state's rights, allowing him to benevolently hand the problem off to each state, averting the heavy hand of the federal government. Framing the issue as protecting states' rights directs attention away from the abortion/choice issue and the need for the leader to weigh in.

Political leaders mobilize their followers through various strategies aimed at generating interest, obtaining buy-in, causing action, and rewarding engagement by delivering on followers' expectations. If effective at conducting these activities, followers may campaign on behalf of the leader, the ultimate measure of mobilization. It may be attending a rally, making a contribution, wearing a branded t-shirt, or placing a bumper sticker on their car. This sort of act not only promotes the candidate but also serves as a statement about the status and values of the follower. In that manner, it will likely expand throughout the follower's network—real life or virtual. Figure 5.1 shows the universally themed messages of each leader's campaigns in simple and direct terms, allowing for individual interpretation sans conflict.

To effectively deal with competing interests, the leader must frame the issue favorably concerning the values driving their followers' behavior. Honesty is paramount. Followers become skeptical if they do not view the leader as a truth-teller. Ironically, for some, being perceived as telling the truth has less to do with the truth than it does with the perception by the follower that the candidate is unafraid to call out a behavior or practice that defies the status quo. When followers perceive the leader as telling the brutal truth—on an issue that may not be popular—they see the leader as authentic, straightforward, and valued. It is someone they want to speak their truth.

Brand awareness is depicted simply and consistently to create recall and identity

Figure 5.1 Campaign artifacts

Think of political correctness—the language, policies, or measures intended to avoid offense—and how people see someone willing to call out political correctness as a leader who is unafraid to "tell it like it is." That person speaks the truth at the street level, where it truly matters to the average American. Followers see that person as discrepant from espousing the party line, thereby someone worthy of their trust. Ironically, that person is seldom punished for their errant behavior; instead, they are given a pass on significant issues because they bravely speak the truth even if the power structure judges them as miscreants. This is a trait that identifies charismatic leaders.

Obama chose to take on the challenge of creating a national healthcare program, a politically sensitive policy that politicians had long sidestepped. He succeeded in passing the Affordable Care Act when the political establishment said it was not warranted or possible. Trump's decision to withdraw the United States from the Paris Climate Agreement in 2017 directly opposed the formally recognized global pact. Both of these actions challenged the norms of political discourse and ultimately positioned these two as courageous leaders willing to take bold action.

This challenge begins with developing a base of support or a core group of passionate followers who believe deeply in what the leader represents. People buy into the leader before they buy into the vision.[25] Charismatic leaders, like Obama and Trump, are typically adept at impression management and, therefore, can execute strategic, communicative, and organizational practices to build a loyal and active group of supporters. Attracting followers is tied to recognizing and developing core issues that resonate most with potential supporters. These pressing concerns affect their daily lives, such as economic stability, healthcare, safety, education, and national security. Understanding these core issues helps the leader tailor their messages and policies. Communicating them with passion moves people to action.

To further this grassroots action, political leaders develop a stump speech. Its purpose is to introduce the candidate and highlight what they stand for and how followers will benefit by lending their support. By articulating clear goals to which followers relate, the message can resonate and lead to action on behalf of the candidate, ranging from contributing time or money to demonstrating support by adopting the leader's emblems of identity (e.g., buttons, hats, t-shirts, bumper stickers, and yard signs) to volunteerism and active participation in the campaign.

A stump speech often includes a comparison with opponents, highlighting differences in policy and vision and arguing why the candidate is a better choice. The speech concludes with a call to action urging the audience to vote, support, and spread the word about the campaign. Stump speeches are crafted to appeal to emotions using rhetoric that connects emotionally while being easily adaptable to different audiences with modifications based on current issues of the moment or audience reactions. They are a fundamental tool in a candidate's campaign arsenal, designed to leave a lasting impression and galvanize voter support.

Charismatic leadership communication is accelerated through use of rhetorical devices

The euphemistic phrase conspicuously posted on a Florida residence

SOURCE: Biosthmors, CC BY-SA 4.0<https://creativecommons.org/licenses/by-sa/4.0>, via Wikimedia Commons

Figure 5.2 Example of a dog whistle communication

Mobilizing support moves beyond stirring the passions of followers. It requires a team and a union between the leader, their inner circle, and engaged followers. Influential leaders surround themselves with competent people dedicated to reaching and engaging prospective followers and building the community's base. In vibrant campaigns, dog whistle messages surface. Consider the "Let's Go Brandon" phrase that grew out of a NASCAR telecast when announcers who were interviewing driver Brandon Brown confused the crowd's chant of "F*** Joe Biden" for "Let's Go Brandon." The result was a new euphemistic code phrase was born (see Figure 5.2).

Even with spirited and engaged followers, the onus of team building is on the candidate to lead the effort, and that means being adept at conducting spirited town halls, rallies, social media posts, traditional media interviews, and other forms of communication. This engagement not only shows that the leader is accessible and attentive to the needs of their potential supporters but also becomes a feedback message for the candidate to sense and measure the reactions to their words and actions. This helps develop a shared identity around their common values or goals. A leader can foster this by emphasizing what unites the potential supporters, such as common goals, shared struggles, or collective aspirations.

With a message and identity in place, setting up a network of volunteers, opening campaign offices, and coordinating efforts to ensure that the message reaches as many people as possible is essential. Mobilization efforts might include voter registration drives, informational campaigns, and rallying events. Maintaining continuous visibility through regular updates, ongoing campaigns, and continuous presence in the media heightens visibility. It helps the leader stay relevant and responsive to the changing dynamics within the various constituencies of the candidate's following.

Finally, addressing the opposition effectively involves defending against attacks, proactively setting the terms of the debate, and staying ahead of the narrative. Effective counter-strategies can reinforce the leader's strengths and expose the weaknesses in opponents' positions. If a leader is willing to evolve strategies based on what is or isn't working, the campaign can maintain momentum, which is crucial to a win on election day.

Agility allows the leader to respond to new challenges and opportunities, energizing the support base and aligning with their vision. Through these steps, a political leader can build a robust and dedicated base of support, which is critical for sustaining a long-term political career and achieving electoral success. These strategies, whether used separately or together, help political leaders mobilize and maintain their followers' support, influencing public opinion and achieving their political objectives.

Presidential charisma in political campaigns and governance

Charisma is challenging to pinpoint. It is more than personal magnetism, more than the warm glow of its presence, and more than a compelling attractiveness or charm that can inspire devotion in others. In a sociological or psychological context, it often refers to a personal quality attributed to leaders who arouse devotion from others. It is rooted in something the follower is passionate about, like the Second Amendment or religious freedom. Suppose the candidate is seen as someone who can advance the cause, defend them from opponents, and accomplish change to improve their lives. Indeed, followers are attracted to that leader and become engaged when the leader appears to be equipped to accomplish something when others have repeatedly failed. In these circumstances, followers bestow the gift of charisma upon the leader. They consider that a person is endowed with unearthly powers, which elevates the leader to another level, transcending the secular world. The gift, whether they know it or not, is charisma.

In modern-day contexts, charismatic individuals are typically seen as possessing exceptional communication skills, a strong sense of vision or mission, and the ability to connect with others on a deep emotional level. Further, it is inextricably tied to the highest levels of power and politics. Examining charisma at the presidential level captures our imagination. A selected review of crucial moments in the successful terms of successful presidents provides lessons on how their charismatic moments may have played a role in their political and governance success (see Figure 5.3).

Peaceful transition of power between the 44th and 45th presidents of the United States

President Obama welcomes President-elect Donald Trump on January 20, 2017 Photo Credit: Jim Watson/AFP

Figure 5.3 Rare photo of two charismatic presidents standing side by side

John F. Kennedy, our 35th US president, captured the imagination of a public primed for bold, new leadership to take the country in a new direction. In his campaign for president in 1960, Kennedy exhibited classic charismatic leadership in attracting and exciting Democratic voters with his head-on approach to challenging the established political forces of the day.

Kennedy entered the national scene after a highly successful and relatively crisis-free post-war Republican Administration. Dwight D. Eisenhower served two terms as president from 1952 to 1960. He arose from one of the traditional sources of leadership development, the military. A West Point graduate, Ike, as he was affectionately known, handily won both of his elections. He focused on containing communism and federal deficits in check, two compelling post-World War II themes. Not considered disruptive, Eisenhower also retained New Deal agencies and expanded Social Security. He was a steady, safe presidential choice for the times. He opposed Senator Joseph McCarthy's aggressive anti-communist suspicion and accusations of American citizens he believed were courting Communism. He sent in federal troops to enforce court orders that integrated schools in Little Rock, Arkansas, and was credited with establishing the Interstate Highway System. History views his presidency as being in the upper tier of American presidents but not charismatic.

Eisenhower's presidency stabilized during significant social, economic, and political change. During economic growth and prosperity, Eisenhower represented calm and stability and focused on maintaining the status quo. Like a responsible father, he saw to the needs of a country that had emerged victorious from a global war, an accomplishment in which he had a significant role. But needs are not wants. Want is a source of motives. This work explores the roots of leadership as the wellspring of want. In his seminal work on the topic—simply titled *Leadership*—James MacGregor Burns (1978) wrote:

> The sources of leadership and followership lie in vast pools of human wants and in the transformation of wants into needs, social aspirations, collective expectations, and political demands. Human beings embody these wants and other motives from birth. At the moment infants are expelled from the calm warmth and dependence of the uterus into the shocking, bewildering world of light and sound, of touching and prodding, of deprivation and fulfillment, they begin the lifelong process of stimulus and response that will culminate for some in skills and motivation for leadership.[26]

By the end of Eisenhower's two terms in the White House, the stage was set for a vigorous campaign between Republican Richard Nixon, then vice president, and the Democrat John F. Kennedy, U. S. senator from Massachusetts. This was the first time candidates for president debated publicly. It also "ushered in a new era in which crafting a public image and taking advantage of media exposure became essential ingredients of a successful political campaign."[27] Analysis of the debate concluded that the two were evenly matched on substance, and to the radio audience, the first debate was considered a draw, with some giving Nixon the edge.

However, for those who watched it on television, "the senator from Massachusetts won over the 70 million television viewers by a broad margin." The Kennedy edge was attributed to his on-air presence,

> staring directly into the camera as he answered each question. Nixon, on the other hand, looked off to the side to address the various reporters, which came across as shifting his gaze to avoid eye contact with the public—a damaging blunder for a man already known derisively as "Tricky Dick."[28]

The real difference? Kennedy was unmistakably charismatic.

However, there was much more to his charismatic style than his charming presence. Kennedy was eager to challenge the status quo and vigorously defend what he believed in, most importantly, himself. Early in the campaign, Kennedy, a Catholic, encountered stiff anti-Catholicism sentiment from rural areas in the South and West, fearing that the pope would rule his presidency.

> Kennedy attacked the problem head-on in a speech to the Greater Houston Ministerial Association, where he stated that if, as president, he found

himself forced to choose between violating his conscience and violating the national interest, he "would resign the office."[29]

This courageous confrontation demonstrated his ability to achieve the outcomes authorized by his followers in his election victory.

Eloquent as he was, his gift of charisma was anchored in his willingness to take personal risks and "engaging in self-sacrificing behavior . . . [or] demonstrating innovative and unconventional behavior."[30] For Kennedy to boldly confront his opposition, he demonstrated authentic, charismatic behavior. To clarify and expand, along with stage presence—an attribute often credited to charismatic people—Kennedy demonstrated three additional charismatic traits: an ability to assess the environment realistically, a willingness to take personal risks, and a willingness to demonstrate unconventional behavior to achieve organizational objectives. In his inaugural address, he set the tone for his presidency that empowered his followers: "Ask not what your country can do for you, but what you can do for your country." This call to empowerment was a common theme of his tenure.

Historically, the country was ripe for a call to take on the challenge of making a better country. After two stable terms under General Dwight D. Eisenhower, Democrats were eager to wrest away the White House. The path was cleared when Kennedy, a young, energetic hero of World War II,[31] emerged as the charismatic leader who commanded respect and pointed the way to the dissolution of the status quo after eight years of Republican rule. Kennedy demonstrated behavior true to charismatic leaders: a desire to change the way of doing things to create a new order. Such leaders are recognized as change agents and, more importantly, benefit by being visible in a beneficial way, accomplished by adept impression management,[32] which compels them to stand out to get attention, whether to themselves or their cause.

Charismatic presidents distinguished themselves through their ability to "influence followers by arousing strong emotions and identification with the leader."[33] In the leadership discussion, scholars believe charismatic leadership is a form of transformational leadership, a kind of leader–follower relationship that is "concerned with emotions, values, ethics, standards, and long-term goals, and includes assessing followers' motives, satisfying their needs, and treating them as full human beings."[34] Both Trump and Obama demonstrate that effect on followers. That is a leader who clearly and forcefully articulates a way to challenge the status quo so that followers adhere to the leader in an extraordinary way and are transformed in the process.

We now understand that charisma in this discussion is not a casual reference to a charming personality or an electrifying speaker. It stands, then, that not every inspiring figure is charismatic. Instead, a much more rigorous set of criteria must apply to deem a leader charismatic. Specifically, followers have much to say about the presence of charisma in a leader, or more appropriately, have much to do in that they advance their concept of self for realizing their true individual identity, known as self-concept.[35] Charismatic leaders effectively connect self-concept with the organization's goals and members' collective experiences.

The charismatic designation was not lightly awarded since Max Weber[36] elevated charisma as one of three types of legitimate authority—the other two being traditional and rational-legal. Further adding to the idea that charisma is an individual gift, Weber determined that charismatic authority is relatively unstable because the authority held by a charismatic leader may not easily extend to anyone else after the leader dies. Further research on the limits of charisma for the charismatic leader includes findings that "charismatic authority is succeeded by a bureaucracy controlled by a rationally established authority or by a combination of traditional and bureaucratic authority."[37] Simply put, it is impossible to sustain charismatic leadership without the charismatic leader.

Charismatic leadership has been scrutinized over the years, partially because it is a complex topic and because its presence is legitimized not only by the leader's behavior but also by the transformation of the follower. From the leader's perspective, follower self-concepts are catalyzed. Outcomes are accomplished through four distinct leader actions: (a) amending (clarifying) follower understanding of the challenge, (b) presenting an appealing vision of the future, (c) illuminating a collective identity and purpose among followers, and (d) empowering individuals and the overall group to accomplish desired outcomes.[38] We will explore these steps more thoroughly in upcoming chapters.

Robert House[39] discovered charismatic leaders could be distinguished by their strong belief in self, a need to influence others, and outsized self-confidence. This, coupled with findings that charismatic leaders can make the challenge before them appear more courageous, morally correct, and significant,[40] explains the unique combination that produces passionate commitment to accomplishing goals. Obama's *Yes We Can* and Trump's *Make America Great Again* slogans stirred the hearts and souls of followers and motivated them to action because the words were backed up by what followers believed was possible from the leader. Trump and Obama turned the wants of their followers into needs that only they could deliver. Further, it occurred when all other options had been exhausted. Each individual's charisma stems from Max Weber's model of pure charisma in that

> there exists among followers some need, goal, or aspiration that is unfulfilled by the existing order . . . [and that] followers submit to the leader, . . . because the leader is seen as the sole possessor of the means for achieving the charismatic promise.[41]

Each leader demonstrated their skills in implementing their unique brand of charismatic leadership.

Barack Obama effectively employed various devices and strategies to mobilize political action during his campaigns and presidency:

- Oratory and Rhetoric: Obama was renowned for his oratory skills. He used eloquent and inspirational rhetoric to connect with people, convey his message, and inspire action. His speeches often featured themes of hope, change, unity, and resilience, resonating deeply with a broad audience.
- Social Media and Technology: Obama's campaigns pioneered their use of social media and technology. His team effectively utilized platforms like Facebook, Twitter, and YouTube to engage with voters, particularly younger demographics, to disseminate his message, organize events, and fundraising. This approach allowed for direct communication with supporters and facilitated grassroots organizing.
- Grassroots Organizing: Obama's campaigns were noted for their grassroots approach, encouraging local volunteer involvement and community organizing. His team empowered volunteers to take ownership of the campaign in their communities, providing them with tools and resources to canvass, phone bank, and organize local events.
- Data-Driven Campaigning: Obama's team used data analytics to target voters and tailor messages effectively. They harnessed data to understand voter preferences, behaviors, and demographics, optimizing campaign strategies to reach and mobilize specific segments of the electorate.
- Inclusive Messaging: Obama's rhetoric often emphasized inclusivity, diversity, and unity. He sought to build a broad coalition of support, appealing to a range of demographics, including young voters, minorities, and cross-party lines. This inclusive approach helped mobilize a diverse base of supporters.
- Narrative Storytelling: Obama effectively used narrative storytelling in his speeches and campaigns to connect with people personally. By sharing his own story and the stories of everyday Americans, he illustrated his points and policies in a relatable and compelling manner.
- Policy-driven Mobilization: Obama linked his call for political action to specific policy goals and reforms, such as healthcare, climate change, and economic recovery. This connection between policy and grassroots activism helped mobilize supporters invested in these issues.
- Community Engagement: Throughout his presidency, Obama continued to engage with communities across the country, holding town hall meetings and public forums. This ongoing engagement helped sustain political action and support for his administration's initiatives.

This ongoing engagement helped sustain political action and support for his administration's initiatives. He drew upon tradition and innovative tactics to mobilize political action and support for Obama's campaigns and policy initiatives, reflecting his adeptness in using various tools to engage and inspire a broad base of supporters.

Donald Trump employed a range of devices to mobilize political action, characterized by his unique approach to communication and campaign strategy:

- Direct Communication via Social Media: Trump distinguished his social media chops by mastering Twitter. He used it to bypass the filter of traditional media. He could then speak in his unique voice in a provocative style that dominated the news cycle, allowing him to share his message unfiltered, rally his base, and dominate the news cycle.
- Populist Rhetoric: In touch with emerging underlying concerns, he appealed to the concerns and frustrations of people who felt ignored by politicians. He focused on "hot-button" issues: immigration, trade, and national security, framing him as a champion of the common man.
- Rallying and Public Events: Trump re-invented the political rally. It was not a gathering; it was a show featuring the fiery rhetoric of the star of the show. These events were extolled as evidence of a movement, engendering a viral happening in the minds of devotees.
- Controversial and Provocative Statements: Trump's colorful, often profane language commanded media attention and moved supporters to see him as a truth-teller. This approach kept him highly visible and solidified his perception of a revolutionary-styled ethos.
- Branding and Personal Image: Development of his personal was ever-present in his well-honed branding practices and reputation management. He used his books, highly visible properties, and his TV persona from *The Apprentice* to create celebrity status. His eponymous catchphrase, "You're fired!" appealed to voters disillusioned with traditional political figures' unending and unfulfilled promises.
- Simplifying Complex Issues: Trump developed an ability to simplify complex issues into sound bites. Slogans like "Make America Great Again" (MAGA) were metaphors evoking skilled use of euphemisms, a figure of speech that softens the otherwise harsh tone of meaning.
- Us versus Them Narrative: Trump leveraged the idea of a binary choice to pit ideas and people against one another. The "us versus them" narrative positions him and his supporters against identified adversaries, political opponents, the media, or foreign entities, fostering a sense of solidarity and action among his supporters.
- Fear and Insecurity: Fear is a motivator, and Trump recognized that people hated losing something they valued the most. By identifying the loss, he could effectively pose as the solution. He regularly fished the headline to accentuate fears of terrorism, crime, and immigration, moving people to action to restore safety and national security.

- Questioning Conventional Wisdom and Norms: In pure charismatic fashion, Trump questioned conventional wisdom. He positioned himself as a disruptor who could bring radical change to Washington, a place he dubbed "The Swamp" appealing to voters tired of the status quo.

Being charismatic leaders, Trump and Obama effectively mobilized political action by engaging directly with supporters, dominating media narratives, and fostering a robust and passionate support base galvanized by their messages and approach, albeit in contrasting styles.

Notes

1 Pierce, C. P. (2015, July 17). Tip O'Neill's ideas that all politics is local is how government dies. *Esquire*. https://www.esquire.com/news-politics/politics/news/a36522/how-all-government-is-local-and-thats-how-it-dies/.
2 Bernays, E. L. (1928/1955). *Propaganda*. New York, NY: Ig Publishing, p. 37.
3 Bernays, E. L. (2011). *Crystallizing public opinion*. New York, NY: Ig Publishing, p. 19.
4 Ibid, (p. 20).
5 Ibid, (p. 21).
6 Ibid.
7 Ibid, (p. 22).
8 Trump executed Executive Order 13769 on January 27, 2017, titled "Protecting the Nation from Foreign Terrorist Entry into the United States," labeled the "Muslim ban" by Donald Trump, commonly referred to as the Trump Muslim travel ban, restricting admission to the country of people from Iran, Libya, Somalia, Sudan, Syria, Yemen, and Iraq. The order was reveres in the courts. https://en.wikipedia.org/wiki/Executive_Order_13769.
9 On August 19, 2016, before an overwhelmingly white crowd in Dimondale, Mich., where 2.8%of the population is African American, then-candidate Donald Trump stumped for black votes. After blaming Democrats and their nominee, Hillary Clinton, for his repeated stereotypical view of African American lives, Trump ended his pitch with a blunt query: "What do you have to lose by trying something new, like Trump? . . . What the hell do you have to lose?" https://www.washingtonpost.com/blogs/post-partisan/wp/2017/09/27/trump-asked-blacks-what-the-hell-do-you-have-to-lose-we-now-have-their-response/.
10 Diaz, D. (2016, September 29). Obama: Why I won't say 'Islamic terrorism'. *CNN Politics*. https://www.cnn.com/2016/09/28/politics/obama-radical-islamic-terrorism-cnn-town-hall/index.html.
11 French, J., and Raven, B. (1959). The bases of social power. In D. Cartwright (Ed.), *Studies in social power*. Ann Arbor, MI: Institute for Social Research, pp. 150–167.
12 Raven, B. H. (1993). The bases of power: Origins and recent developments. *Journal of Social Issues,* 49(4), 227–251. https://doi.org/10.1111/j.1540-4560.1993.tb01191.x.

13 Heifetz, H. A. (1994). *Leadership without easy answers*. Cambridge, MA; London, UK: The Belknap Press of Harvard University Press, p. 20.
14 Ibid.
15 Burns, J. M. (1978). *Leadership*. New York, NY: Perennial, p. 12.
16 Kovach, M. (2020, July). Leader influence: A research review of French and Raven's (1959) power dynamics. *The Journal of Values-Bases Leadership*, 13(2). https://scholar.valpo.edu/cgi/viewcontent.cgi?article=1312&context=jvbl.
17 Burns (1978), (p. 20).
18 Heifetz, R., Grashow, A., and Linsky, M. (2009). *The practice of adaptive leadership: Tools and tactics for changing your organization and the world*. Boston, MA: Harvard Business Press, p. 89.
19 Ibid, (p. 307).
20 Ibid, (p. 18).
21 Ibid, (p. 19).
22 Ibid, (p. 114).
23 Ibid, (p. 115).
24 Ibid, (p. 305).
25 Maxwell, J. C. (2007). *The 21 immutable laws of leadership*. Nashville, TN: Thomas Nelson Publishers.
26 Burns, J. M. (1978). *Leadership*. New York, NY: Harper Row; Perennial.
27 History.com.editors. (2019, June 10). *The Kennedy-Nixon debates*. https://www.history.com/topics/us-presidents/kennedy-nixon-debates.
28 Ibid.
29 Hamby, A. L. (2017). How Kennedy's charisma won the white house. *The Wall Street Journal (New York, NY)*.
30 Conger, J. A., and Kanungo, R. N. (1998). *Charismatic leadership in organizations*. Thousand Oaks, CA: SAGE, p. 73.
31 In his Pulitzer Prize winning book *Profiles in Courage* (1955), Kennedy wrote about individuals who had taken unpopular stands in defending the ideals of America at different times in the nation's history. Written as a junior senator from Massachusetts, the book drew attention to Kennedy who was then recognized as a war hero responsible for rescuing his crew after their PT boat collided with a Japanese destroyer.
32 First conceptualized by Erving Goffman in *The Presentation of Self in Everyday Life* (1959), impression management is a conscious or unconscious process that people use to influence the perceptions of others by controlling information in social interactions. https://en.wikipedia.org/wiki/Impression_management.
33 Conger and Kanungo (1998), (p. 14).
34 Northouse, P. G. (2022). *Leadership: Theory and practice* (9th ed.). Thousand Oaks, CA: SAGE.
35 Shamir, B., House, R. J., and Arthur, M. B. (1993). The motivational effects of charismatic leadership: A self-concept based theory. *Organizational Science*, 4, 577–594.
36 Weber, M. (1921/1978). *Economy and society: An outline of interpretive sociology*. Berkeley, CA: University of California Press.
37 Turner, J. H., Beeghley, L., and Powers, C. H. (1995). *The emergence of sociological theory* (6th ed.). Boston, MA: Cengage Learning.

38 This finding is rooted in the works of a host of research from Csikszentmihalyi, M., and Rochberg-Holton, E. (1981). *The meaning of things: Domestic symbols and the self.* Cambridge, UK: Cambridge University Press; Kinder, D. R., and Sears, D. O. (1985). Public opinion and political action. In G. Lindzey, and E. Aronson (Eds.), *The handbook of social psychology.* New York, NY: Random House, pp. 659–742; Prentice, D. A. (1987). Psychological correspondence of possessions, attitudes, and values. *Journal of Personality and Social Psychology,* 53(6), 993–1003; and Snyder, M., and Ickes, W. (1985). Personality and social behavior. In G. Lindzey, and E. Aronson (Eds.), *The handbook of social psychology*. New York, NY: Random House, pp. 883–847.

39 House, R. J. (1977). A 1976 theory of charismatic leadership. In J. G. Hunt, and L. L. Larson (Eds.), *Leadership: The cutting edge*. Carbondale, IL: Southern Illinois University Press, pp. 189–207.

40 Shamir, House, and Arthur (1993).

41 Bradley, T. B. (1987/1999). *Charisma and social structure: A study of love and power, wholeness and transformation.* New York, NY: toExcel, p. 33.

Reference List

Bernays, E. L. (1928/1955). *Propaganda.* New York, NY: Ig Publishing.

Bernays, E. L. (2011). *Crystallizing public opinion.* New York, NY: Ig Publishing.

Burns, J. M. (1978). *Leadership.* New York, NY: Harper Row; Perennial.

Diaz, D. (2016, September 29). Obama: Why I won't say 'Islamic terrorism'. *CNN Politics.* https://www.cnn.com/2016/09/28/politics/obama-radical-islamic-terrorism-cnn-town-hall/index.html.

French, J., and Raven, B. (1959). The bases of social power. In D. Cartwright (Ed.), *Studies in social power.* Ann Arbor, MI: Institute for Social Research, pp. 150–167.

Heifetz, H. A. (1994). *Leadership without easy answers*. Cambridge, MA; London, UK: The Belknap Press of Harvard University Press, p. 20.

History.com.editors. (2019, June 10). *The Kennedy-Nixon debates.* https://www.history.com/topics/us-presidents/kennedy-nixon-debates.

Kovach, M. (2020, July). Leader influence: A research review of French and Raven's (1959) power dynamics. *The Journal of Values-Bases Leadership,* 13(2). https://scholar.valpo.edu/cgi/viewcontent.cgi?article=1312&context=jvbl.

Maxwell, J. C. (2007). *The 21 immutable laws of leadership.* Nashville, TN: Thomas Nelson Publishers.

Pierce, C. P. (2015, July 17). Tip O'Neill's idea that all politics is local is how government dies. *Esquire.* https://www.esquire.com/news-politics/politics/news/a36522/how-all-government-is-local-and-thats-how-it-dies/.

Raven, B. H. (1992). The bases of power: Origins and recent developments. *Journal of Social Issues,* 49(4), 227–251. https://doi.org/10.1111/j.1540-4560.1993.tb01191.x.

6 The bright and dark sides of charisma

Benefits and risks of charismatic leadership

The bright side of charisma is experienced in its capacity to mobilize people toward positive change. Charismatic leaders are visionaries. They effectively articulate a vision of the future that captures the imagination and spirits of their followers. They communicate emotionally uniquely, generating outsized trust and loyalty through conviction and passion. Such leaders can catalyze social movements, drive innovation, and inspire collective action to overcome significant challenges. Their magnetism is a unifying force, and when combined with a deft skill of impression management, effectively bridges diverse groups to achieve common goals by instilling a sense of purpose and identity among their constituencies.

However, the potency of charisma can cast long shadows, revealing its dark side. When charisma is harnessed for self-serving ends or without regard for ethical considerations, it can become manipulative and dangerous. Left unchecked, charismatic leaders may exploit their influence, blinding followers to their flaws. This further suppresses dissent, centralizing power in an inner circle of trusted operatives expected to carry out the leader's orders. The dark side of charisma is often characterized by a tendency to foster cults of personality, punish those who become disloyal, and pursue goals that benefit the leader over the collective well-being. In extreme cases, this can lead to demagoguery, where a leader's persuasive ability exploits societal divisions, spreads propaganda, and consolidates authoritarian power.

The bright and dark characteristics may co-occur in the leader. However, over time, a pattern emerges. The dual nature of charisma demands a nuanced understanding of its power. When coupled with integrity, empathy, and a commitment to the greater good, charisma can be a formidable force for positive impact. Yet, when divorced from these principles, it can lead to manipulation, coercion, and societal harm. The dichotomy of charisma thus presents a paradox in the study of leadership and social influence. Concerning followers, it can ignite the flame or stoke the fires of discord. As with all potent phenomena, scrutiny under a watchful eye is warranted.

DOI: 10.4324/9781003463047-7

Exploration of how different segments of the population viewed each leader

The recurring theme of this book is that these two leaders differ significantly in how they communicate, see the world, and attract, engage, persuade, and motivate followers. Each represents different forms of charismatic leadership—personalized and socialized—and in their own way, each possesses the means to identify and inspire followers to achieve their unique shared vision. Through personal example, risk-taking, empowering followers, effectively exercising impression management, evident goal-setting abilities, inspiring trustworthiness, and the means to motivate, their followers willingly authorize them to achieve their desired outcomes. Finally, each, in his way, creates uncommon loyalty and commitment from followers.

The bonds between a charismatic leader and their followers are often intense and personal, characterized by a mutual sense of passion and commitment. These leaders are adept at creating a solid emotional connection with followers, inspiring them to pursue a collective vision intensely. Their personal magnetism, communication skills, and conviction often foster deep-seated loyalty and high trust among their followers. These relationships can transcend traditional leader–follower dynamics, with followers feeling a sense of personal identification with the leader's goals and values and, therefore, developing an intense need to be a part of the cause to form a strong bond with the leader. This bond is further strengthened by the leader's ability to make followers feel valued and understood, creating a powerful, shared sense of purpose and destiny.

The population segments that may support a high-level leader like the President of the United States typically span a broad spectrum, depending on how the president crafts and communicates their policies, party affiliation, and leadership style. As in all political situations, segments can be binary in various categories. Individuals are driven to align or not align with one of the binary choices in each category. Typically, followers cluster on one side or another—Democrat, Republican, or Independent, for example—in each segment listed below. Or, they may be split ideologically as conservatives, moderates, or liberals.

Further, individuals may reflect a blend, labeling themselves as conservatives on some issues, liberal or progressive on others, or moderates. Below are segments where followers will break based on their beliefs and how leaders can position their candidacies. Consider the following segments:

- Party Loyalists: Members of the president's political party are often core supporters, rallying behind shared ideologies and party platforms.
- Issue-Oriented Supporters: Individuals who strongly believe in specific issues (e.g., abortion, immigration, healthcare, economy, and environment) may support the president if his actions align with their priorities.

- Business Community: Business leaders and entrepreneurs may support candidates if their policies promote economic growth, deregulation, and business-friendly tax codes.
- Labor Unions and Workers: If the president advocates for labor rights, higher wages, and job security, this can garner support from unions and the working class. While there may be a split between union and non-union members, they are generally aligned around economic and workplace quality issues.
- The Military and Veterans: A president who supports robust military funding and veterans' services may be supported by service members, defense contractors, and veteran communities.
- Educational Institutions and Students: If the president focuses on education policies, student loan reform/relief, and research funding for specific ideological causes, these groups may support or not support based on their situation.
- Marginalized Communities: If the president champions civil rights, anti-discrimination measures, and social justice, support may come from racial, ethnic, LGBTQ+, and other marginalized groups; they will curry favor from affected individuals.
- Religious Groups: Presidents who reflect specific moral values or policy positions that align with religious teachings or beliefs may find strong support among specific faith-based communities.
- Geopolitical Allies: Internationally, allied nations may support the president if his foreign policies and diplomacy strengthen or serve their economic and security issues.
- Cultural and Ideological Sympathizers: People who identify with the president's cultural background, personal story, or ideological outlook may also be supportive.
- The General Public: Depending on the president's overall performance, particularly in handling national crises, segments of the general population may offer support due to perceived competence, charisma, or trustworthiness.

Presidential support often fluctuates based on current events, policy outcomes, and shifting public opinions. These factors are subject to the leader's management practices. For the charismatic, researchers have determined potential liabilities (see Figure 6.1). Presidents typically work to maintain a coalition of these segments to uphold their mandate and achieve their policy goals. Further, these groups are subject to the president's abilities to position, persuade, and endear themselves to followers, and with the extraordinary capabilities of Trump and Obama. The outcome of support may be nudged in one direction or the other based on the psychological and emotional effects the president exerts, as well as their management practices (see Figure 6.2).

Understanding charismatic leadership from the leader-follower interplay persective

Contextual: The group faces a challenge so as to thrive.

A leader emerges by effectively signalling both the urgency and need for intragroup coopertion.

Since leadership potential is difficult to observe, followership is spurred by cues the leder exhibits, such as:

- External factors embedded in the environment (e.g. instability, unrest)
- Physical cues (appearance, facial features, formidability)
- Social cuse (reputation, networks size, signaling abilities)

As such, charisma is best understood as the result of the interplay between followership, context, and cues.

Leader Cues: The charismatic leader signals their availability and willingness to swiftly mobilize group action through cues that demonstrate their ability to lead. They:

- Attract attention through their outsized energy and nonverbal traits such as facial expressions or appearance
- Arouse emotions through speech and actions
- Articulate a gripping vision that closely aligns with follower beliwefs and identity
- Evoke efficacy as the first mover—if you see it first, you must be equipped to fix it
- Inspire group cohesion to realize their hopes and dreams

Inspired by Grabo, Spisak, & vanVugt (2017)

Figure 6.1 Graphic depiction of charismatic leadership

Potential liabilities in the charismatic leader's management practices

- Poor management of people network, especially superiors and peers
- Unconventional behavior that alienates
- An autocratic, controlling management style
- An informal/impulsive style that is disruptive and dysfunctional
- Claims of responsibility for innovative products and ideas when in reality the sources are other individuals
- Alteration between idealizing and devaluing others, particularly those who report directly
- Creation of excessive dependence on themselves among subordinates
- Failure to manage essential details and to act as an effective administrator
- Attention to the superficial
- Absence from operations
- Failure to develop successors of equal ability

Conger & Kanungo, 1998 SOURCE: Adapted from Conger (1990, p. 52)

Figure 6.2 The potential downside to charismatic leadership

Examination of the psychological and emotional effects of charismatic leadership on followers

Donald Trump commanded a unique and often polarized standing among various segments of the American population during his tenure as president and after that. Through his robust interpersonal dynamics, he exhibited several psychological and emotional effects, often defaulting to the dark side in building his base of support. Trump referred to his followers as a movement with a robust support base mostly centered on conservative ideology, particularly among those aligned with his America First ideology and approach to governance.

Followers saw in Trump a strong leader equipped to fight for them to restore the country to traditional values, best expressed as their grievances and opposition to globalism, gun control, government overreach, abortion, and immigration. His loyalists were drawn to his direct and often confrontational style and appreciated his honesty and refreshing contrast to typical political discourse. However, opponents saw the dark side of his persona.

His presidency was frequently marred by accusations of gaslighting, a psychological tactic where the perpetrator seeks to make others doubt their perception of reality to gain power or control. This characterization stemmed from various actions and communication styles exhibited by Trump during his time in office. Trump's tendency to deny observable facts was at the heart of these accusations. A prime example just hours into his term was the controversy over the crowd size at his inauguration. Despite photographic evidence to the contrary, Trump and his administration insisted that the attendance was record-breaking, challenging the public's trust in empirical evidence.

The dissemination of misinformation was a recurring theme throughout his tenure. He often made either partially misleading or entirely false statements about a range of issues, from economic statistics to the severity of the COVID-19 pandemic. This relentless spread of inaccuracies created an environment where truth became fuzzy or needed more definition, making it challenging for the public to discern factual information.

Trump's relationship with the media further exemplified his gaslighting tendencies. He frequently branded mainstream media outlets as "fake news," notably when they reported critically on his actions or policies. This tactic sowed distrust toward established news sources and endeavored to position Trump as the primary arbiter of truth, undermining objective reality in favor of his narrative. Moreover, Trump's approach to historical events often involved rewriting past occurrences to suit his preferred narrative better. This revisionism extended to his reinterpretation of international relations, domestic policies, and even his previous statements and conduct, further blurring the lines between historical accuracy and fabrication.

Perhaps his most steadfast act of gaslighting occurred in his insistence that the 2020 election was stolen and that widespread voter fraud occurred; even after state and federal election officials, including those appointed by Trump himself, confirmed the election's integrity, Trump continued to assert that the election was fraudulent. More importantly, his followers fell in line with his accusation. A CNN poll fielded throughout July 2023 reported, "Republicans and Republican-leaners say [President Joe] Biden's win was not legitimate, up from 63%" earlier in the year (Agiesta and Edwards, 2023).

Trump deftly employed euphemism, a word or phrase used to soften the harshness of a literal meaning. Closely related to this practice is the term "dog whistle," which refers to language that conveys a particular message to a specific group of people, often carrying a hidden or coded meaning while appearing innocuous or unrelated to the uninitiated. For example, his use of the term "law and order," which on the surface could be seen as a call for reducing crime and enforcing laws, was a coded appeal to followers with concerns about racial unrest and protests, particularly in the context of the Black Lives Matter movement and civil unrest in cities like Ferguson and Baltimore. Trump cleverly used these figures of speech to convey a message with a wink and a nod, a device to bring followers closer to the inner circle through inclusive language based on shared beliefs.

There is ample evidence that Trump generated outsized commitment from his followers, especially evidenced in two incidents involving his messaging interpreted to invite followers to threaten violent action in defense of Trump and his tenuous assertions. The events surrounding his role on January 6, 2021, in summoning and stirring followers to disrupt the Congressional certification of the 2020 election resulted in more than a thousand people being arrested, with more than 700 pleading guilty and more than 150 "convicted of at least one charge at a trial decided by a judge or a jury" (Albarracín, 2015). Three months prior, Trump failed to

> condemn white supremacists and their role in violence in some American cities . . . [in the wake of protests of the George Floyd killing] branding it solely a "left-wing" problem and telling one far-right extremist group to "stand back and stand by" (Durkin Richer and Kunzelman, 2024).

While the violence in these two examples is not gaslighting, the events preceding the violence explain how gaslighting played a role in the context of the events.

Trump switched parties to run for president. However, he far exceeded expectations anyone may have had of his effect on the GOP. Trump methodically reshaped the Party by energizing specific issues he determined to be emotional hot buttons, such as immigration, foreign trade, crime, and economic stability. Unlike his well-loved predecessor, Ronald Reagan, a quarter of a century before, Trump re-imagined the party, inserting his image as representative of a departure from the glory days, not simply fashioning himself to fit the expectations of the party faithful.

Reagan promised a vibrant city on a hill, a metaphor of "a tall, proud city built on rocks . . . God-blessed, and teeming with people of all kinds living in harmony and peace" (Frum, 2021). Trump re-positioned the vision with the phrase "Make America Great Again" (MAGA), meaning a return to a past state where his supporters believed America was more prosperous, powerful, respected, and ultimately a safer place to live. Reagan's GOP vision was built on pride, inclusion, and possibility, whereas Trump's was built on fear.

Fear is a survival tactic. Like all animals, humans are equipped with a survival instinct when they sense danger. It is called the fight-or-flight instinct, and it triggers a physiological response when stress from an impending threat to safety occurs. Fear can be used to move people to action. For example, in the workplace, leaders often invoke a sense of urgency by making a business case that the firm and its people are in a crisis unless they act. In *Leading Change*, his seminal book on change management, John Kotter wrote of the necessity of leaders to establish a sense of urgency to cause followers to act:

> To lead a change effort and gain the cooperation of necessary stakeholders, the first step leaders must take is to create a sense of urgency. It requires clear and honest communications that create a sense of urgency rather than a sense of doom (Kotter, 2012).

While Kotter's advice hinged on creating a sense of urgency related to logical and moving arguments, Trump's take was to invoke fear, a much more direct route appealing to followers' emotions. There is little doubt that fear is a motivator. According to a meta-analysis conducted by researchers who tested multiple predictions about the effect of fear, they repeatedly found, "Fear appeals are effective at positively influencing attitude, intentions, and behaviors . . . there are few circumstances under which they are not effective" (Ronyne and Kunzelman, 2020).

Trump regularly intoned the message of fear to followers through simple, direct messages, like suggesting the 2020 election was stolen, and with his opponent, Joe Biden, as president, the country would fall into chaos and disaster, losing its greatness forever. This narrative created a sense of urgency and existential threat among his supporters, propelling them to rally behind his candidacy to reclaim control from the alleged corrupt elites. By framing the situation in such stark terms, Trump effectively utilized fear as a catalyst for action, convincing many voters that drastic measures were necessary to avert a looming catastrophe for the nation. When leaders consistently play on fear to motivate their followers, they are considered dissonant leaders.

Just as in its musical origins, dissonance is a lack of harmony. In most cases, dissonant leaders are short-lived; they destroy the spirit of people and wear them down, leading to work avoidance. However, some dissonant leaders are "more subtle, using a surface charm or social polish, even charisma, to mislead and manipulate. Those leaders either don't truly hold their professed values, or they lack empathy, caring about little other than their advancement" (Tannenbaum et al., 2015). The term that describes this behavior is demagoguery. While rare in business,

> politics seems the demagogue's more natural ecological niche . . . [when] leadership built on . . . cultivating fear or hatred of some "enemy"—[it] amounts to a cheap trick, a quick and dirty way to mobilize a group toward a common goal.

Looking back on Trump's takeover of the GOP, he laid the groundwork for his vision a year before his campaign commenced, when he signaled his distaste for the Reagan *shining city on a hill* metaphor. In a 2014 interview, he warned of brandishing American exceptionalism as hypocritical and offensive to world leaders who believe it to be bragging. While it may seem disingenuous for a man prone to hubris, this was a swipe at elites and a calculated means to contrast his stance, in a more significant cause, protection of the people: "Well, I think it's a hazardous term in one way because I heard Putin saying, 'Who do they think they are, saying they're exceptional?'"

In this manner, Trump expresses the discrepant view, the perspective most people gloss over because they are captivated by Reagan's oratory. But by raising these arresting thoughts—like challenging a GOP icon like Reagan—Trump captures the imagination in a straightforward and uncomplicated manner, and that resonates with souls who believe it takes a contrarian, especially one with the tools to play in a rough game, to cure their country's woes. Trump effectively undermined the Reagan vision, only to replace it with his own.

As we examine these two presidents' emotional and psychological effects, it is essential to understand the impact charismatic leaders may have had on their followers. Specifically, it is beneficial to review how researchers have theorized the effects of socialized and personalized leaders concerning motives, needs, influence, outcomes, and values (see Figure 6.3).

Barack Obama's presidency was characterized by a diverse coalition of support that evolved over his two terms. He, too, had a profound psychological and emotional effect on his followers. His cool and measured leadership style and eloquent oratory resonated deeply with Americans searching for change in a hopeful manner. The onset of the Great Recession, the ongoing Iraq War, and the aftermath of Hurricane Katrina were all perceived to be a failure of leadership by the previous administration at the outset of the 2008 campaign.

Further, voters witnessed, and some were personally affected by, the collapse of the mortgage industry through dubious lending practices. Katrina was a multifaceted disaster, highlighting inept emergency preparedness, socio-economic inequality, and failed government responsibility. One of the enduring images of the event was President George Bush's fly-over of the city in Air Force One, leaving the impression of the president as a curious observer, not a protector or rescuer of the people.

The spectrum of charismatic leadership—from Socialized to Personalized

	Socialized Charismatic *Positive Form*	***Personalized Charismatic*** *Negative Form*
Underlying motive	*Altruistic (intent to benefit others)*	*Egotistic (intent to benefit self)*
Manifest needs	*Affiliative interest* *Institutional power* *Social achievement* *Self-discipline/self-development*	*Affiliative assurance* *Personal power* *Personal achievement* *Self-aggrandizement*
Influence strategy	*Empowerment*	*Control*
Leader objective in terms of behavioral outcomes in followers	*Emphasis on internalization of vision by changing followers' core attitudes, beliefs and values*	*Emphasis on compliance behavior and identification with the leader*
Moral values and influence	*Ethical*	*Unethical*

Adapted from Kanungo & Mendonca, 1996 SOURCE: Conger & Kanungo, 1998

Figure 6.3 Key dimensions of charismatic leadership

Political conditions were ripe for a leader to interject a bright outlook for the country. During his ascent to the presidency, Obama's message of hope and change was fueled by many factors that resonated deeply with the American people. Leading up to the 2008 election, the palpable dissatisfaction with the prevailing political and economic landscape set the stage for acceptance of Obama's socialized charisma style and its emotional and psychological effects on followers. His oratory skills projected a message followers found energizing.

His vision of a united America was embedded in the psyche of potential followers four years before his nomination in a message reaching beyond the divisions of partisan politics, "There's not a liberal America and a conservative America; there's the United States of America."[1] His message underscored themes of unity, shared values, and the common hopes of the American people, resonating widely and establishing him as a significant figure in the Democratic Party yearning for a new direction and leadership.

Obama drew upon his well-developed emotional intelligence to present a confident and steady demeanor. In 2009, Congressman Joe Wilson (R-SC) "shocked many observers when he shouted, 'You lie!' after the presidents denied that health care legislation would provide free coverage for illegal immigrants."[2] Obama remained calm and mindful and relied on the reaction from others to tamp down the change and re-position it as a baseless claim. John McCain, among others, came to his rescue in calling out Wilson for being out of line. It was a clear example of Obama's command of emotions. There is evidence from researchers that emotions are contagious. And that the human brain is an open system capable of sharing emotions and, ultimately, feelings and moods.

> We are literally "wired" to pick up on subtle clues from one another—and therefore, in a sense, we are dependent on one another for our emotions. We gauge our emotional response on the feelings we notice in the people around us.[3]

We look for facial expressions and tone of voice that may be fleeting but "important signs of the emotions that drive behavior."[4] Obama's face was often expressive, displaying a range of emotions from concern and seriousness when discussing grave matters to joy and relaxation during lighter moments. This expressiveness made his speeches and interactions more dynamic and impactful. However, he was very aware of how he was portrayed in the media. In the early days, he said that most photos and news footage

> showed me active and smiling . . . my facial expressions exuding energy and command. Now that most of the stories were negative, a different version of me appeared: older-looking, walking alone along the collonade . . . my shoulder slumped, my eyes downcast, my face weary.[5]

Amidst this backdrop of uncertainty and disillusionment, the economic strife in the latter half of the decade, including the housing market collapse and a looming financial crisis, Obama engendered a sense of urgency and a demand for change. His promise of a new path forward was a beacon of hope to those grappling with job losses, foreclosures, and the broader ramifications of economic instability. Obama's promise of change, his embodiment of inclusivity, and his desire to break from conventional political paradigms set him apart.

His background, demeanor, and rhetoric of unity and inclusiveness spoke to a diverse electorate seeking a positive psychological perspective. A significant part of his self-management was rolled up under the heading of positivity, called the growth mindset. He said, "We highlighted what I stood for rather than what I was against. I policed our tone from top to bottom."[6] His penchant for impression management delivered early results in the campaign, upon which he capitalized to cement his hope and change message into the voter's psyche.

After his surprise loss to Hilary Clinton in the 2008 New Hampshire primary, Obama drew upon inspiration from his 2004 Senate race to generate resilience and energize his staff and supporters, all demoralized by the setback. He revived a three-word phrase and incorporated it into his speech using an effective rhetorical device called anaphora—methodical repetition—to emphasize his message. "Yes, we can," he repeated, driving home his conviction in his vision for the country. Obama told his supporters, "We know the battle ahead will be long, but always remember that no matter what obstacles stand in our way, nothing can stand in the way of the power of millions of voices calling for change."[7] This speech was about the resilience needed in the campaign and a broader call to action for change and improvement in America. He continued, "When we've been told that we're not ready, or that we shouldn't try, or that we can't, generations of Americans have responded with a simple creed that sums up the spirit of the people: *'Yes, we can.'*"[8] It highlighted his ability to inspire and mobilize people around a positive vision for the future. It had such an impact that the crowd began spontaneously chanting, Yes, We Can.

The spontaneous response to a speaker, such as that experienced by Obama in his post-primary loss, is called collective effervescence, coined by Émile Durkheim in his century-old theory of collective assemblies and collective effervescence. "For Durkheim, individuals' survival and well-being rest on cultural resources and social belonging that must be revived periodically in collective assemblies . . . in his attempt to clarify how these assemblies achieve this revitalization."[9] Modern researchers discovered, "Ample support also exists that because shared emotions are increasingly amplified in collective context, they can fuel high-intensity experiences."[10]

The study findings confirmed what Durkheim theorized, that a sense of energy, harmony, and unity experienced by individuals in a group during rituals or shared events led to a heightened sense of togetherness and solidarity. The chanting represents a collective emotional response, where individuals in the crowd connect with the speaker and each other, reinforcing their shared values, beliefs, and identity. In this context, the bond is emotional, as it taps into shared feelings and passions, and cognitive, as it reflects a shared understanding and acceptance of the speaker's ideas. The spontaneous response is generated by the bond within the relationship.

The political climate of the time, characterized by intense partisanship and division, further amplified the desire for a leader who could transcend political discord and foster bipartisanship. Obama's approach to bridging divides and his call for collective action offered a refreshing contrast to the prevailing political dynamics. The empowerment and active engagement that Obama championed, grounded in his roots as a community organizer, had a catalytic effect on the political landscape. His call for civic participation galvanized a diverse array of individuals, from seasoned activists to previously apathetic citizens, inspiring them to take an active role in shaping their community's and country's future. This movement toward greater civic involvement fostered a sense of individual agency and collective responsibility.

Adding to the momentum was the historic nature of Obama's candidacy. His potential to become the first African American president ignited a sense of possibility and progress, mobilizing a wide array of voters, particularly young people and minority communities, and infusing the campaign with historical urgency. As discussed in this work, central to Obama's appeal was his charismatic leadership and exceptional oratory skills, which enabled him to connect with Americans on a deeply emotional level, turning his campaign into a movement that transcended traditional political boundaries.

Moreover, when America's international reputation was challenged, Obama's global perspective and commitment to restoring the country's standing through diplomacy and international cooperation struck a chord with those who valued a more engaged and positive American presence on the world stage.

The confluence of these elements, combined with a strategically organized campaign that leveraged new media and grassroots organizing, cultivated a potent appetite for Obama's vision of hope and change. This groundswell of support ultimately propelled him to a historic victory in 2008, followed by his re-election in 2012, marking a defining era in American political history.

Concluding thoughts

Emotionally intelligent leaders "build resonance by tuning into people's feelings—their own and others'—and guiding them in the right direction."[11] Obama demonstrated high levels of what Daniel Goleman called Emotional Intelligence: self-awareness, self-management, social awareness, and relationship management.[12] This prepared him to consciously impact his followers' emotional and psychological well-being, resulting in a powerful alliance for change. Donald Trump generated unprecedented passion and loyalty among his followers. He demonstrated the raw power of his emotions and proved to be an extraordinary manager of his persona.

Barack Obama's tenure, marked by efforts to enact sweeping reforms amidst a climate of significant challenges, attracted passionate supporters and detractors, reflecting the complex tapestry of American politics and society. On the opposite end of the spectrum, Donald Trump's command of the significant power structure enabled him to stall legislation, shift the judicial system to the far right, and ensconce himself as an enigmatic leader.

Notes

1 Cited from his 2004 speech to the Democratic National Convention four years prior to his nomination.
2 Nadler, R. S. (2011). *Leading with emotional intelligence: Hands-on strategies for building confident and collaborative star performers*. New York, NY: McGraw-Hill, p. 89.
3 Boyatzis, R., and McKee, A. (2005). *Resonant leadership*. Boston, MA: Harvard Business Review, p. 23.
4 Elkman, P. (2004). *Emotions revealed: Recognizing faces and feelings to improve communications and emotional life*. New York, NY: Henry Holt.
5 Obama, B. (2020). *A promised land*. New York, NY: Crown Books, p. 538.

6 Ibid, (p. 539).
7 Ibid, (p. 110).
8 Ibid.
9 Rimé, B., and Páez, D. (2023, February 8). Why we gather: A new look, empirically documented, at Émile Durkheim's theory of collective assemblies and collective effervescence. *Perspectives on Psychological Science*, V18(6). https://journals.sagepub.com/doi/abs/10.1177/17456916221146388.
10 Ibid.
11 Goleman, D., Boyatzis, R., and McKee, A. (2013). *Primal leadership*. Boston, MA: Harvard Business Review Press, p. 46.
12 Ibid, (p. 32).

Reference List

Agiesta, J., and Edwards, A. L. (2023, August 3). CNN poll: Percentage of Republicans who think Biden's 2020 win was illegitimate ticks back up near 70%. *CNN Politics*. https://www.cnn.com/2023/08/03/politics/cnn-poll-republicans-think-2020-election-illegitimate/index.html.

Albarracín, D. (2015). Appealing to fear: A meta-analysis of fear appeal effectiveness and theories. *Psychological Bulletin,* 141(6), 1178–1204. https://doi.org/10.1037/a0039729.

Boyatzis, R., and McKee, A. (2005). *Resonant leadership*. Boston, MA: Harvard Business Review.

Durkin Richer, A., and Kunzelman, M. (2024, January 5). Hundreds of convictions, nut a major mystery is still unsolved 3 years after the January 6 Capitol riot. *The Associated Press*. https://apnews.com/article/election-2020-joe-biden-race-and-ethnicity-donald-trump-chris-wallace-0b32339da25fbc9e8b7c7c7066a1db0f.

Frum, D. (2021, January 1). Is America still the 'shining city on a hill?'. *The Atlantic*.

Goleman, D., Boyatzis, R., and McKee, A. (2013). *Primal leadership*. Boston, MA: Harvard Business Review Press.

Kotter, J. (2012). *Leading change*. Boston, MA: Harvard Business Review.

Nadler, R. S. (2011). *Leading with emotional intelligence: Hands-on strategies for building confident and collaborative star performers*. New York, NY: McGraw-Hill.

Obama, B. (2020). *A promised land.* New York, NY: Crown Books.

Rimé, B., and Páez, D. (2023, February 8). Why we gather: A new look, empirically documented, at Émile Durkheim's theory of collective assemblies and collective effervescence. *Perspectives on Psychological Science*, V18(6). https://journals.sagepub.com/doi/abs/10.1177/17456916221146388.

Ronyne, K., and Kunzelman, M. (2020, September 20). Trump to far-right extremists: 'Stand back and stand by'. *The Associated Press*. https://apnews.com/article/election-2020-joe-biden-race-and-ethnicity-donald-trump-chris-wallace-0b32339da25fbc9e8b7c7c7066a1db0f.

Tannenbaum, M. B., Hepler, J., Zimmerman, R. S., Saul, L., Jacobs, S., Wilson, K., and Albarracín, D. (2015). Appealing to fear: A meta-analysis of fear appeal effectiveness and theories. *Psychological Bulletin,* 141(6), 1178.

Index

For Product Safety Concerns and Information please contact our EU representative GPSR@taylorandfrancis.com
Taylor & Francis Verlag GmbH, Kaufingerstraße 24, 80331 München, Germany

www.ingramcontent.com/pod-product-compliance
Lightning Source LLC
LaVergne TN
LVHW010938110826
845149LV00013B/2653

* 9 7 8 1 0 3 2 6 1 3 0 6 2 *